YOUNG PEOPLE'S STORY OF
OUR HERITAGE

YOUNG PEOPLE'S
STORY OF
OUR HERITAGE

THE ORIENT

by

V. M. HILLYER and E. G. HUEY

New Edition Designed and Revised by Childrens Press, Chicago

Consultants

William T. Nichol, Principal
Charles Gates Dawes Elementary School, Evanston, Illinois

John R. Lee, Professor of Education
Northwestern University, Evanston, Illinois

Meredith Press, New York

Illustrations in the order in which they appear

Contents

Acknowledgments

Cover painting, top: Cranes stretch their long necks in flight
John Hollis—Hollis Associates

Cover painting, bottom: An isolated Pacific coast
Nita Engle—Hollis Associates

Page 2: Scene of Suva, Fiji
Quantas Empire Airways Limited

Frontis: Night shot of Hong Kong
British Overseas Airways Corporation

Opposite: The Australian koala bear
Australian News and Information Bureau

Designer: John Hollis

Project Editor: Joan Downing

Manuscript Editor: Mary Reidy

Editorial Staff: Frances Dyra, Gerri Stoller

THE ORIENT,

Australia, and the South Sea Islands

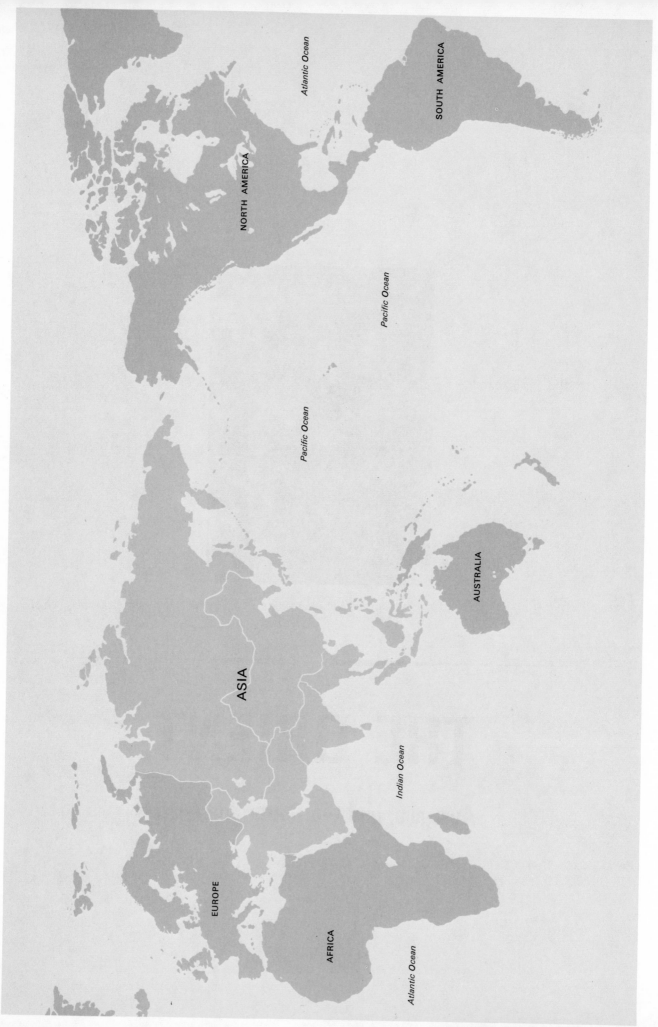

The Orient, Australia, and the South Sea Islands

The largest continent in the world is Asia. In this book we will learn about part of this continent—about what some of the countries of Asia are like. We will learn also about the smallest continent in the world and about some of the smallest, but most important, islands.

The part of Asia we will find out about in this book is called the Orient. To Western people, the Orient is the most interesting and colorful place in the whole world. Nearly everything in the Orient is very different from what it is in the Western world —printing, sculpture, music, poetry, and even ways of living and thinking.

The smallest continent in the world is Australia, a country all by itself. Australia is not part of the Orient. Its people are more like Europeans or Anglo-Americans, for the continent was settled by the British. New Zealand is near Australia, and it, too, was settled by the British. The traditions in both of these places are *occidental*. Occidental means the opposite of *oriental*. The people of the Western world are occidental. The people of the Orient are oriental.

left: World map showing the five divisions of Asia

11

The islands of the South Pacific are yet another part of the world that we will find out about in this book. These islands are like little patches of Paradise. People from the Western world have always thought longingly about someday seeing or living in the islands of the South Pacific. In this book, we will try to explain why this is so.

You can see that we will learn about many very different places and many very different people. This book is really like three books in one. The first book is about part of Asia—the Orient. The second book is about Australia and New Zealand. The third book is about some of the islands in the South Pacific.

Look at the map and find these parts of the world. See how far they are from Europe and how much farther away they are from the New World. Look at how big Asia is.

Now look at the map of Asia; the one that shows how the continent is divided into regions. We can divide Asia into five regions called Northern or Soviet Asia, Eastern Asia, Southwestern Asia, Southern Asia and Southeastern Asia. Northern, Eastern, and Southeastern Asia are the parts we will read about in this book. Many of these lands are islands and sometimes they are grouped together and called Insular Asia. Insular means island and many of these islands are important countries.

Russian Republics are found in Northern Asia. The largest one, the Russian Soviet Federated Socialist Republic is also called Siberia. The others are Kazakh, Turkmen, Uzbek, Tadzhik, and Kirghiz Soviet Socialist Republics. The Mongolian People's Republic is an independent country in Northern Asia.

Eastern Asia includes China, Taiwan, North and South Korea, Japan, and Hong Kong. China takes up the major part of this area.

Many countries make up Southeastern Asia, and some of these are very small. Burma, Thailand, Cambodia, Laos, and North and South Viet Nam cover most of the mainland of Southeastern Asia. At the tip of the land is Singapore. Malaysia includes part of the mainland and some of the surrounding islands. Other islands form Indonesia and the Philippines.

---

right: Northern Asia, Eastern Asia, and Southeastern Asia

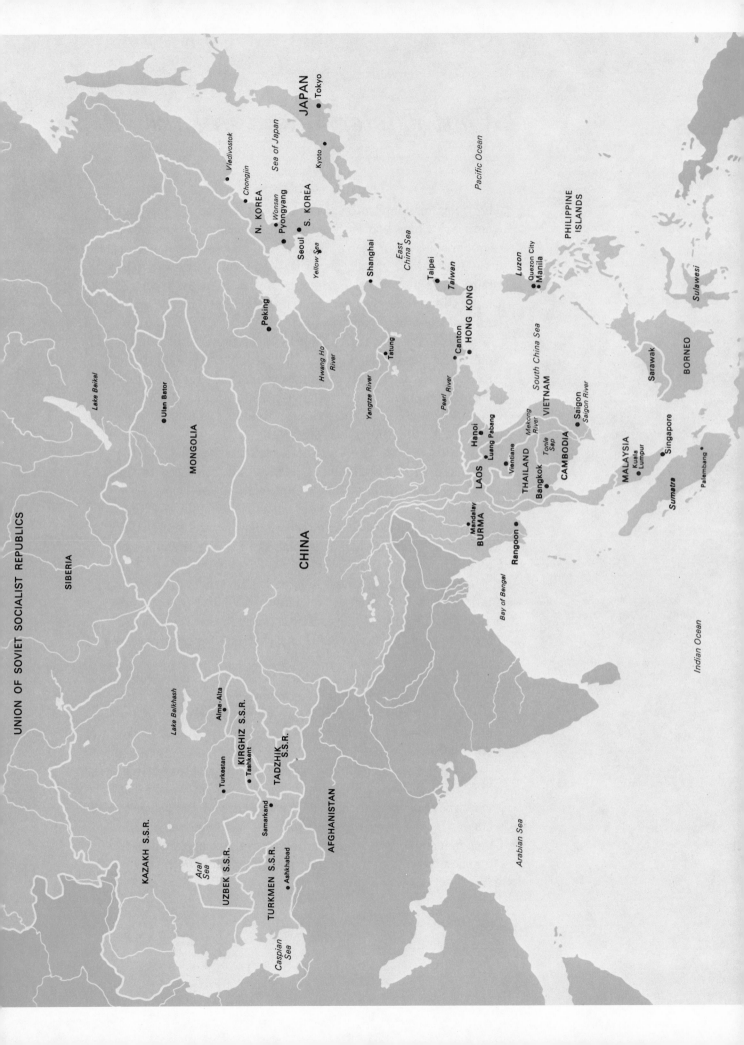

What Eastern Asia is Like

The whole mainland of eastern Asia is occupied by only two countries—China and Korea. But China has nearly the entire region. Look at your map of eastern Asia and see just how very little Korea has. Notice also the island called Taiwan (tie-whan). It is also called Formosa. Taiwan is really a part of China. China today has two governments. One is on the mainland and the other is on Taiwan.

Just before World War II, China was a republic. But Chinese Communists had been fighting the Republic for some time. After World War II, the Communists won that fight and established a Communistic form of government on the mainland of China. They called it the Peoples' Republic of China, even though it is not really a republic at all.

The Nationalists, who wanted to keep the republic, lost the civil war with the Communists in 1949 and retreated to the island of Taiwan. The Chinese Nationalists kept their form of government and its name, the Nationalist Republic of China. Many of the nations of the world recognize only the Nationalist Republic of China. Others recognize the Peoples' Republic of China.

About ten million Chinese live in Taiwan. But about seven hundred million live on the mainland of China! Many more people live there than in any other country in the whole world. There are so many people in China that one person in every four in the whole world is Chinese.

China must be a very big country to hold all of these people, of course, but it is not the biggest country in the world. It is the third biggest. The U.S.S.R. which is the country of the Russian people, is the largest country, and Canada is the second largest.

When there are as many people in a country as there are in China, feeding them is a problem unless the land is so good that it can produce a lot of food, or unless there are a lot of things to trade for food. So you will want to know just what the land in China is like and just what kind of natural resources it has to offer these seven hundred million people who live on it.

---

right: Map showing eastern Asia

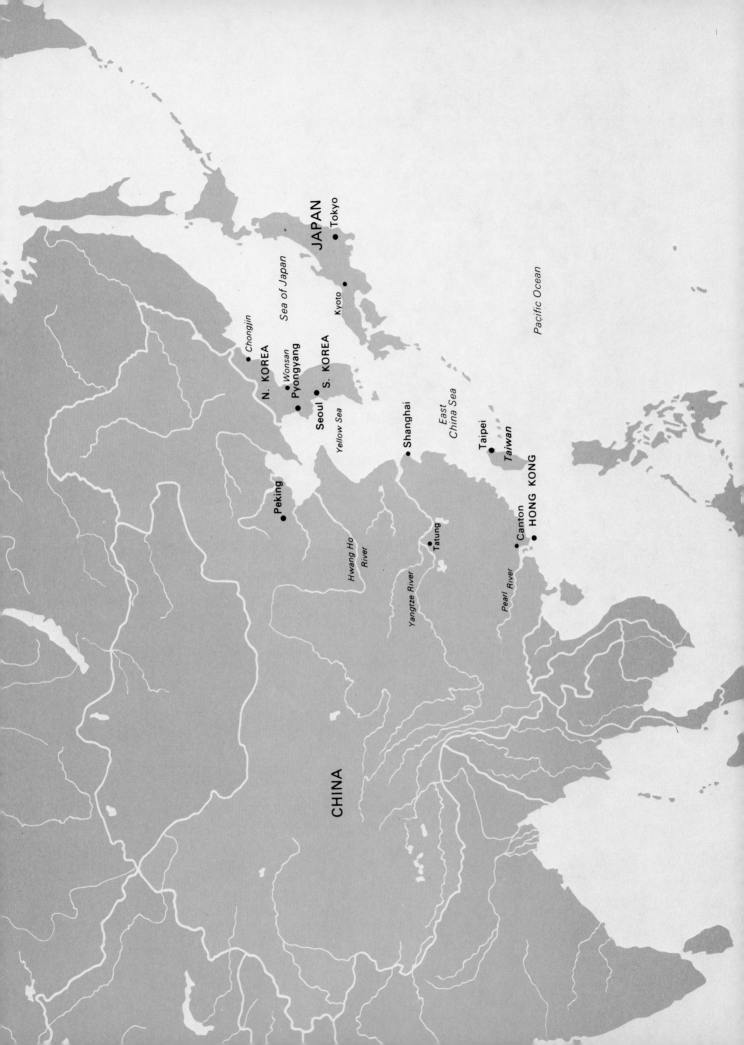

In its different kinds of land and climate, China is more like a continent than like a country. We can think of this giant land as being divided into three parts—north, south, and west. Both the north and south have land and climate that are good for growing things. In the north, crops like wheat and soybeans and barley do well. In the south, rice does well. Rice is very important to the diet of the Chinese. In fact, it is the main food in much of Asia.

Much of the western region is really wasteland, where no farming of any kind can be done. But it is good land for grazing, so livestock do well there.

Much of the land in China is hilly, not suited for farming. China does raise a lot of food, but not enough for its tremendous number of people. What would seem like great food production anywhere else is too little in China.

As far as natural resources go, China is not altogether lucky either. There are great stores of coal, but still not enough. The iron China has is of poor quality. Other minerals it has, like tungsten and tin, are the ones called secondary minerals because they are not the most valuable to the modern world.

China has five things that help it and three that work against it. The five things that help it are its size, its weather, its traditions of farming, its coal reserves, and the background of its people. Because it is so big, China does have a lot of resources. If these are not always of just the right kind for the modern world, at least they are something that the people can use.

The weather in China is varied, but the growing season is long enough and the moisture is great enough to make farming possible in the cultivated land and to give the people something of their own. Even the cold winters are a good thing because a variety in climate always seems to make people more ambitious and hardy and progressive.

Only the United States has more coal than China. You know how important coal is to industry. There are many things China does not have that are important to industry, too, but these things can be traded. So China can perhaps become an industrial nation when it has to.

China's traditions of farming have been fortunate. It has been a great agricultural land for many hundreds of years, but the Chinese have not worn out the land because they have learned how to preserve it.

left: Rice fields are found throughout the country of China

The Globe and Mail, Toronto—Photo by Charles Taylor

17

The fact that the Chinese are one people instead of a mixture of many groups has helped them, too. They have one culture and so are less divided than are some other peoples who have many cultures within the boundaries of their countries.

Three things that are problems in China have really held the country back. These things are isolation from other countries, the rugged land, and the tremendous population. For many centuries, China was isolated from the rest of the world. Long before European countries had developed civilization, China had made great progress. But it kept to itself. In fact, it did not want the Western world to know anything about it and it did not want to know anything about the Western world. That was fine for a while. But the Western world progressed beyond the Oriental world. The Chinese, particularly, still believed they were superior and that people from the Western world were savages—and they felt there was nothing to learn from savages.

By the time the modern world had come into being, the Chinese were still backward in many things that now have become important to them. Only recently have they become interested in learning from the rest of the world, especially in the area of science.

The tremendous population is China's biggest problem. Food is in such short supply that the Communist government must ration it in order to give all the people a share. And the people do not get as much food as they need, because there really is not enough to go around.

Korea has problems, too, but they are of a different kind. Korea is like Belgium, in that it has become the battlefield of other nations. The nations are Russia and the countries of the free world.

After World War II, Russia attempted to influence Korea to become Communistic. The free world did not want this and a great conflict arose. The two sides fought over Korea and finally the dispute was settled by compromise. Each side gave in a little and agreed to divide the country in half. The northern part of the country is the Democratic People's Republic of Korea, which is guarded by Russia, and is Communistic in government. The southern part is the Republic of Korea, which is democratic and is guarded by the countries of the free world.

The southern part of Korea (South Korea) is mostly a rice-growing country. The northern part (North Korea) is mostly a wheat- and barley-growing country. Each half of the country needs both kinds of food, really, and must rely on foreign powers to provide what it cannot produce for itself.

The Land and People of China

Even if you never go to China, you can see things that are Chinese. Other countries have admired China for many, many years, and museums display Chinese things. One of the first things you might notice in China or in Chinese sections of museums is the strange writing. It doesn't go across the page from left to right. It doesn't go across the page at all. The Chinese start on the top right-hand corner and go down to the bottom and then back up to the top. Their writing is in columns. They do not use an alphabet, but delicate-looking symbols called *characters* that they make with a soft brush. Chinese characters were first like *hieroglyphics*. A picture was drawn to represent a word. Later the pictures were combined to make other words. All these were finally changed to what is used today. These characters stand for certain one-syllable sounds, and there are thousands of them. Today the Chinese have a new and easier alphabet that is being used in schoolbooks, and perhaps the written language will become easier to learn.

Cups and saucers, plates and platters we call "china" because they were first made in China. Silk material for women's dresses and men's ties comes from China, and so does tea. Other things that we believe first came from China are printing, the compass, gunpowder, goldfish, firecrackers, and varnish.

Jade is a very strong mineral that comes from China. When jade was first mined, it was made into useful utensils, but the Chinese knew jade was too precious for ordinary things, and they used it to make beautiful objects. Most jade that we find is a greenish-white or grayish-green. It looks like a kind of marble. It is not a very hard substance but it wears very well. Jade cups were used by Chinese emperors many hundreds of years before the birth of Christ. Jade ornaments are worn by people to bring them good health. Even today, if the jade loses its luster or breaks, it is thought to bring bad luck. Children are given bracelets or anklets made of jade for good luck.

Tea has been used in China for many centuries. It was first used by the Zen Buddhist priests to keep them awake when they were praying. A book about tea and the preparation of

A Buddhist priest praying

tea was written about 780 A.D. After tea was brought into Japan it became very popular because of the ceremony surrounding its use.

As we mentioned, for many centuries the Chinese kept to themselves and had their own culture. But in the last century China has been changing and adopting new things like electric lights, railways, automobiles, and airplanes. China used to be ruled by an emperor. In those days, the men wore their hair in a long braid that reached to their waist or knees, or even to the ground. We call such a braid a pigtail. The Chinese called it a *queue*. When China became a republic, many of the Chinese in the cities cut off their queues; but in the towns and country some still wear them.

Chinese gentlemen used to let their fingernails grow four or five inches long. They never cut them, and to prevent them from breaking off, they put gold cases on them. Such long fingernails were a sign that the person who had them did not work, that he was a gentleman. The longer a man's fingernails, the finer the gentleman he was, for laborers who worked with their hands could not have long fingernails.

Most Chinese worship Buddha and follow the teachings of Confucius. Confucius is a man who lived about 500 years before the birth of Christ. His life was dedicated to helping all the people. He wanted lower taxes, lighter punishments for criminals, and war only if it were absolutely necessary. Confucius taught his ideas to many younger men, and he is thought to be the first private teacher in China. He believed the Chinese idea that the family is very important, that everyone must respect and love his family and never do anything to injure the name of his family. He believed that all mankind was one big family. Confucious taught that by helping others you really are helping yourself, because you make the world a better place.

All over China there are statues of Buddha. People pray in front of the statues. Near the city of Tatung are the Buddha Caves of Yun Kang. Here, in a cliff, man-made caves were carved a few centuries after Christ was born. Inside these caves were placed statues of Buddhas, and above the entrances openings like windows were made. From the outside you can see gigantic statues looking out the windows as you walk along. Buddhist monks used to come here to pray to these images and some even lived in caves that were also cut out of the cliff.

A banquet in China might begin with tea; then would be served things like sweet-and-sour pork, beef cooked in different ways, beans, bamboo shoots, radishes, seaweed, all types of

above: The cormorant is very important to the fisherman in China

fish including shark and shrimp, rolls and cakes. The meal would end with soup made of fish, chicken, or octopus. The ordinary people of the Peoples' Republic of China, unfortunately, do not eat wonderful meals like this. Remember we said that most of the food is rationed? This means each person is allowed to buy only a certain small amount. The food that is not rationed is too expensive for most people to buy. The Chinese eat everything, whether rice or stew, with two sticks called chopsticks.

The Chinese have very little meat, but plenty of fish. They sometimes use a bird called a *cormorant* to catch fish for them. This bird is very greedy and very fond of fish. The fisherman goes out in a boat, puts a ring around the cormorant's throat and lets him out on a string. When the bird sees a fish he dives for it and catches it in his beak. But he can't swallow it because of the ring around his neck. The fisherman pulls him in, takes the fish away, and lets the bird out again. When the cormorant has caught a sufficient number of fish, the fisherman takes the ring off his neck and lets him catch a fish for himself.

21

The Chinese work very hard and have very little money. They have to be very economical. Many of their crops are ruined by droughts, or dry spells, and by floods, too. They live on little food and patch their clothes, because even if they could afford to buy material, there isn't enough to go around. Some of the material produced is sold to other countries.

About a hundred years ago, only one city in China, called Canton, was open to outsiders. Canton is on the Pearl River. When we say "on" we usually mean "by the side," but in Canton many of the Chinese actually live *on* the river—in boats. Boats are lifetime homes of these people, and many of them are born, grow up, and die on the boats without having spent much time ashore. The main part of Canton is, of course, on the land; but the houses are packed so closely together there is no room for regular streets. There are crooked alleys winding and twisting in and out and back and forth, so that a stranger entering the city without a guide would quickly lose his way and be quite unable to get out of the city again.

North of Canton, on the East China Sea, is the city of Shanghai. Before the Communists took over China, Shanghai was so busy as a seaport filled with foreign boats, traders, and businesses that it was sometimes called the New York of China. After the Communists took over, it was very difficult for foreigners to live in Shanghai so most of them had to leave. Shanghai is near the mouth of the Yangtze (yang-see) River, which is the longest river in Asia.

The western part of China is mostly plateaus and mountains. The principal rivers of China start in these highlands and flow east into the Pacific Ocean. The Yangtze has its source in these mountains and so does another river farther north called the Hwang Ho. It winds and twists to the ocean from there. The Hwang Ho is one of the few rivers in the world that has to be drawn differently every time a map is made, for like a live snake it changes. It twists and turns from time to time, and each time it does so, it floods and washes away houses and fields. Recently, the government has tried to control it by building hydroelectric power plants, but they have not been completely successful. Hydroelectric power plants make electricity with the power made from rushing water.

The Hwang Ho is also called the Yellow River. The mud colors it and the blue ocean becomes yellow at the place where the Hwang Ho enters it. That part of the ocean is called the Yellow Sea because of the color. Before land is sighted, the crew of a ship can tell by the color of the water that it is near the mouth of the Hwang Ho.

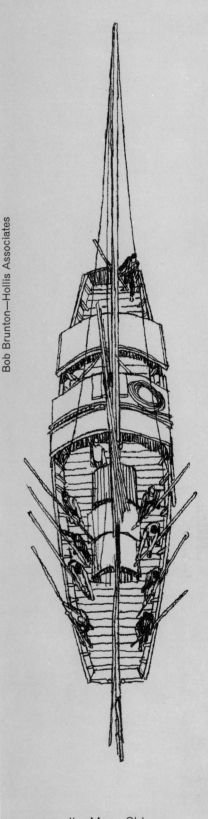

Bob Brunton—Hollis Associates

opposite: Many Chinese villages are very poor

above: Chinese laborers rowing a boat upstream

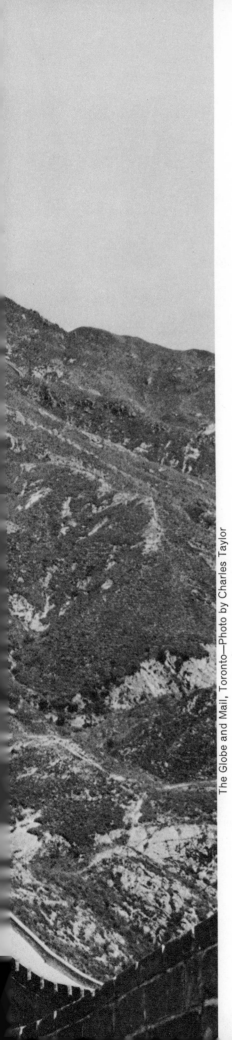

The Globe and Mail, Toronto—Photo by Charles Taylor

Connecting the Hwang Ho and the Yangtze rivers is a long canal called the Grand Canal. It is one of the longest canals in the world. Everywhere in China there are canals, for canals have been the railroads of China, and only recently have there been real railroads. Instead of trains the Chinese use boats called junks, with tall sails and eyes painted on the front so that the boat can "see" its way. For many years the Grand Canal was not navigable because of the *silt* that had settled. Silt is made up of small pieces of earth, clay, or sand that the river collects from its banks as it flows along. If enough is collected, the river or canal becomes so shallow that traffic cannot safely pass through.

Most maps do not show man-made things because they are too small. Even cities are only dots on a map. But on the map of China two man-made things are shown. One is the Grand Canal and the other is a Great Wall across the north of China. The Great Wall has been called the eighth wonder of the world. It was built in the days before Christ was born, when the Chinese used bows and arrows to keep out wild tribes from the north. The wall starts at a big rock in the sea and goes up and down across the land for about 1500 miles. It is from fifteen to thirty feet high and is as wide as a road. In fact, on top of it there is a road. About every two hundred yards there is a watchtower. Much of the Great Wall is in ruins now, but another wall separates China from the rest of the world. This wall is invisible, like the iron curtain. It is called the *bamboo curtain*. Though it is not a real wall, it is very effective in keeping people from entering or leaving China.

Peking is a very old city in the northeastern part of China. It is the capital of China and the largest city. Large factories and universities are in this ancient city. Peking really is two

left: The Great Wall stretches across the north of China

above: The Forbidden City once was the imperial palace of China

walled cities. The inner city has the Forbidden City, government buildings, temples, and parks. The outer city contains the business section and the Temple of Heaven and the Temple of Agriculture.

The Temple of Heaven is now a museum visited by hundreds of people every day. But not too long ago, when there was an emperor of China, no one but the royal family and their court could go into this temple. Every year the emperor and his court would come to the Temple of Heaven in the summer and pray for a good harvest. Visitors now may see the Forbidden City, which contains the palaces of the emperor.

The clothes worn by the Chinese look something like loosely fitting pajamas. They wear pants and jackets or blouses. To see the elegant robes once worn by the emperor and his court, you must visit the Peking Opera Company. Here, singers perform some of the old Chinese music dramas and wear jeweled headresses, exotic make-up and brocaded silk gowns.

Taiwan, a Small Island Country

In Hong Kong you can stand on Mt. Victoria and look into the harbor; in Japan you can stand in a valley and see Mt. Fuji; in Taiwan you can stand on mountains and look down onto the sea. Like a high wall, or cliff, the land on the southeast side of Taiwan rises almost straight from the sea so that there are no beaches or ports—a thrilling sight.

Taiwan is sometimes called Formosa, which is a Portuguese word meaning beautiful. Before the Communists gained control of the mainland, Taiwan had a population of people called Taiwanese. Some Chinese lived in Taiwan then, but since the Nationalists were forced to leave the mainland, about two million Chinese people have fled to Taiwan to live in the Republic of China. Here on this small island the free Chinese try to live and to help other Chinese people live in a free society.

This island country is not very far from the mainland where the Peoples' Republic of China is. In fact, it is only about a hundred miles away. There are two important seaports in Taiwan. They are Keelung in the north, and Kaohsiung in the south. In both of these ports, freighters from many countries dock.

Taiwan has a subtropical climate, which means that things grow there all year round. There is no season when it is too cold to grow things. Of course, the mountains have snow, but that is because they are so high. On the coastal plain, crops grow all year round. Rice is planted in hillsides, called terraces, that look like big steps. Pineapples are grown on plantations and fishing is done all year round.

When we think of China, we think of both the mainland and Taiwan. The Communists would like to control both places. The Nationalists, with their government on Taiwan, would like to bring all the Chinese under a free government. Although two different governments control two areas, there is only one China, which includes the mainland and the islands.

The Nationalists are working very hard to become prosperous. Many light industries have been started on Taiwan and have grown since the land became a republic. Sugar refineries are very important there, too, especially for trading with other countries. Pineapple canning and tea packing are

opposite: A lake near Taipei, Taiwan

---

right: Pineapple harvesting in Taiwan

---

below: Fishing with nets in Taiwan

Consulate General of China

Consulate General of China

Traditional Chinese operas can be seen in Taiwan

also important. Beautiful Chinese pottery and porcelain are made and hand painted by the people there. Porcelain is china that is made of a very fine white material, so fine you can almost see through it. Silk also is produced in Taiwan.

Some of the animals found in Taiwan are black bears, flying foxes, bats, and wild boars. Snakes live in tropical and sub-tropical climates, and many kinds of snakes live in Taiwan. About a dozen of these snakes are poisonous. Leather products, like wallets and belts, are made from snakeskin.

In Taipei (tie-pay), the capital city of Taiwan, there are some ancient castle walls. Many of the people from China live in the capital city and housing is very scarce, but the government is busy trying to build houses for all the people living in the city.

The opera, which originated in China, can be seen in Taiwan. For someone who is accustomed to seeing European opera, the Chinese opera seems very different. In European opera, the audience knows by the scenery whether the setting is in a house or a palace or outside in the forest. Many European operas tell sad stories which have unhappy endings. The first noticeable difference in Chinese opera is the absence of scenery. On the stage there may be just a table and a few chairs. The table may represent a table or it may be a mountain. The chair may be a throne or when put on top of the table it may be a walled city.

The makeup in the Chinese opera is used to show whether a person is good or bad. It can make a face look happy, sad, kind, or mean. The most evil-looking faces are on the warriors who do acrobatics and look very vicious. The music is very different from European music; it is sung or chanted with a different tone, rhythm, timing, and tempo, and sounds very high-pitched and strange to Western ears.

Most Chinese operas have happy endings. Although you may not understand what is being sung, it is easy to understand what is happening.

The New Year's celebration in Taiwan is very colorful and exciting. People greet each other on the street and wish happiness and prosperity to neighbors and friends. Dragon dances and firework displays top off this joyous New Year's celebration.

The British Colony of Hong Kong

Another island very near the mainland of China is important to people who do not want to live under Communism. This island is Hong Kong. Strangely enough, the island does not belong to the Chinese at all but to the British. In fact, it is a British Crown Colony. Because so many Chinese have come to live on the island, the British needed more land in the area of Hong Kong. So they rented Kowloon, on the tip of the Chinese coast, from the Chinese Government. Kowloon is just across the harbor, so close that it takes only seven minutes by ferry boat to get there from Hong Kong.

How do you suppose the British happen to have a Crown Colony right within one of the main parts of China? Well it all started because Europeans wanted to trade with China a very long time ago, during the time of the emperors. Do you remember we said that the Chinese thought other people were barbarians and that they really did not want to have anything to do with them? Well the British, like other Europeans, did want to have something to do with the Chinese. They wanted to trade with them for cotton, tea, and silk. They were not permitted to go to many parts of China, but they were permitted to go to the southern part, to a place called Canton. They could not go anywhere they wanted to go in Canton, but they could stay in the coastal regions. The British also were permitted to take on water at the island that was later to be called Hong Kong.

In order to make trade easier, the British introduced opium to the Chinese. That was the one thing the Chinese wanted that the British had. The Chinese Government did not want their people to have opium, because it is a harmful drug. So a war, called the Opium War, started between the Chinese Government and the British. The British won the war and kept Hong Kong. They have it even today.

Now Hong Kong is a wonderful port in the area where much of the world's trade by ships is carried on. The British have made Hong Kong an important place to world trade. Their chief interest in Hong Kong is in the money it brings them. But they have been forced to have another interest, too—an interest in the millions of refugees who have fled from the mainland to live in Hong Kong. How to feed and house these people is a great problem.

opposite: The fishing village of Aberdeen, Hong Kong

English is the official language of Hong Kong, but more Chinese is spoken than English because most of the people who live in Hong Kong are Chinese. Although Hong Kong, with the small islands nearby that make up the colony, is very small, more than three million people live there. Most of Hong Kong is hillside and swamp, so the majority of the people live in the harbor area.

Victoria Harbor is one of the world's best natural harbors. It is always filled with ships—freighters and luxury liners from every part of the world. Many people make their home on the water, living in the boats they use for fishing. These boats, junks and sampans, have delicate looking sails.

There is some heavy industry in Hong Kong. Shipbuilding and ship repairing are important there. But the island also has light industries, such as textile mills, metal production, and battery manufacturing. Cotton is one of the most important textiles produced in Hong Kong.

Victoria, the capital of Hong Kong, lies along the harbor for about five miles. Rising almost directly from the harbor is Mt. Victoria, called "The Peak." A tram with bright green cars will take you to the top from where you can get a beautiful view of the harbor below. Even if you cannot really see and hear all the bustle going on, you can imagine it when you see all the ships docked. You can look in the other direction and see the green islands spreading throughout the South China Sea.

Steps go up the steep hills from the harbor. There are hundreds and hundreds of these steps and on either side of them there are small shops where tourists especially like to go. Tourism is a very important industry in Hong Kong because so many ships dock in the harbor. Many visitors come ashore from these ships—businessmen, sailors, and vacationers. Hotels, sightseeing guides, buses, restaurants, night clubs, and shops operate with the visitor in mind. They try to make things exciting and pleasant for tourists and make a profit too.

One of the things nearly every visitor goes to see in Hong Kong is Tiger Balm Garden. This is not like an ordinary garden. Instead of lovely flowers to look at, it has figures or scenes that tell stories from history or Chinese mythology, and they preach a lesson. The sculptures are very colorful, and many think they are not very beautiful. Tiger Balm Garden

opposite above: Junks in the harbor in Hong Kong

opposite below: The President Roosevelt ocean liner lies at anchor in the harbor

Quantas Empire Airways Limited

American President Lines Photo

is named after a medicine. Tiger Balm is supposed to be able to cure just about anything. The man who first made and sold this medicine, Aw Boon Haw, became a millionaire by selling the medicine—which may or may not cure the things it is supposed to cure. One of the things he did with the money he made was build the Tiger Balm Garden.

Tourists are always interested in finding good restaurants, and Hong Kong has many of them. Very little food is grown in Hong Kong. There is just not enough land there to produce all the food needed for the people who live and visit there, so most of it has to be imported. It is very good food, and the restaurants are expert at cooking it. In Hong Kong restaurants serve dishes from many parts of the world. Some restaurants are floating restaurants in the harbor. The Sea Palace is one of the largest floating restaurants in the harbor of Aberdeen, the fishing center of Hong Kong. Visitors to the floating restaurants can choose their fish for dinner from a tank if they wish. Chinese food includes such wonderful dishes as sweet-and-sour pork, diced chicken with walnuts, and tiny shrimp cooked in many different ways.

In the shops you can look for all of the treasures that Columbus and the others wanted to find. They include jade, brocade, pearls, ivory, and precious stones. If you have enough time you can have clothes made from beautiful silks and tweeds by Hong Kong's expert tailors.

Throughout the year there are colorful festivals in Hong Kong. The Chinese New Year excites viewers with firecrackers and street parades. The Fishermen Festival has lion dances. The Dragon Boats Race features long canoes with many paddlers, each team trying to win the race.

A visitor to Hong Kong will also hear tales about the pirates of old and might even be shown the coves where the pirates would hide before they went after ships filled with treasures. Tales are told, too, about the smugglers and dope peddlers who sell illegal goods.

North and South Korea

Korea is across the Yellow Sea from China and was first settled by the Chinese. Much of Korea's culture and many traditions were taken from the Chinese.

Korea has not been left to itself for as long as China has. It has been controlled by other countries for many, many years. In the fifteenth century Korea was independent and progressed very well. It was then that the city of Seoul was built. This is the capital of Korea. The Korean alphabet came into being at that time, too.

After that period, Japan tried many times to conquer Korea, and finally in 1910, it did gain control of the country. Japan wanted to make Korea just like its own country, so the people had to change their names to sound like Japanese names, they had to speak Japanese, and they couldn't follow their national customs anymore. Many Koreans left after Japan gained control and went to other countries to live.

After World War II, the country was divided into two parts, using a parallel as a boundary line. When you look at a map, you can see lines drawn across it. You know these lines are not on the earth, but are just drawn on a map. These lines are called parallels. The equator is halfway between the poles and divides the globe into the northern and southern hemispheres. The equator parallel has the number zero. From the equator, lines are drawn all the way up and all the way down. All these lines are numbered too. If you find the equator on a map and follow the parallel lines going up, or north, you will probably be able to find a line numbered forty. Just below forty, you can guess, would be the 38th parallel. This is the line that was used to make a boundary line cutting the country of Korea into two parts.

This was an easy way to divide the country and Russia took the northern part and the United States the southern. They were the occupying powers. The purpose of an occupying

above: The ancient city gate in Seoul, Korea, is one of the few remainders of the past

power is to get the government working again—socially, politically, and economically.

Soon these parts became two separate countries. The northern section was named the Democratic People's Republic of Korea and the southern section the Republic of Korea. Usually they are referred to as North Korea and South Korea.

In 1950 the North Korean army came across the 38th parallel and invaded South Korea. This was the beginning of a struggle that lasted three years, until an armistice, or agreement, was finally signed.

South Korea has many mountains and only a small part of it is good for farming. Most of the people do farm, although they have very small pieces of land. On most of the farms rice is grown. The people live in little towns in clay huts with straw roofs. They wear cotton clothes and sandals made of straw or paper. They lead very simple lives.

Seoul, which is still the capital of South Korea, was first built as a walled city. The wall disappeared long ago but three of the ancient gates are still standing. These gates look more like buildings than gates, though there is an opening through which you can pass.

After the battles with North Korea, there wasn't much left of the city of Seoul. So much fighting was done in the city that thousands of children had lost their fathers and many more children were orphans. Orphanages were built to take care of these children. Many other new buildings had to be built, but still there is not enough living space for all the people. There are large modern buildings in Seoul now, and very few reminders of the past.

Near Seoul is the Han River, which is large enough for boat traffic. Not far from Seoul is the mouth of the Han River, where it empties into the Yellow Sea.

Korea is a peninsula pointing into the Yellow Sea and the Sea of Japan, and it has wonderful fishing waters. Some of the fish caught are hairtail, horse mackeral, cuttlefish, croaker, and anchovy. Much of the fresh catch is exported, but some of it is processed and used as dried fish or made into oil.

North Korea has most of the industry—chemical plants, steel foundries, and textile mills. Mountains run through North Korea, where the highest peak, Paektu san, is over 8000 feet high. The winters are very long and terribly cold. Coal and gold are mined.

The capital of North Korea is Pyongyang. Some say this city was built about 2000 years ago. This old city has been attacked many times, so very few old buildings remain.

The major ports in North Korea, Chongjin and Wonsan, are both on the Sea of Japan.

Both North and South Korea are very poor countries. The people live in very poorly constructed houses, and have little to eat and little to wear.

Japan, The Land of the Rising Sun

When the world was young and people believed in sea serpents, they used to say there was a huge sea serpent a thousand miles long in the sea near China. Wherever the humps on the sea serpent's back stuck out of the water they looked like islands, and whenever the sea serpent twisted or turned in his age-long sleep the islands would shake. Yet, long ago people from China went to these islands on the sea serpent's back and made their homes there, in spite of the fact that he was squirming in his sleep. We now know that these islands are simply old volcanoes in the water, most of which have burned out, and when they shake, as they still do almost every day, we know that the shakes are just earthquakes. We call these islands on the sea serpent Japan and the people Japanese.

The Japanese, however, don't call their island Japan; they call their country of islands "Nippon" which means the Land of the Rising Sun. Of course, the sun rises in other lands too; but when the Japanese went to Japan it was, for them, the land where the sun rose. So their white flag has on it the picture of a red sun.

Though the Chinese and the Japanese both belong to the same race, they are different in many ways. The Japanese are quick learners and quick to copy, and have adopted many things from the Chinese—their way of writing, Buddhism, and eating with chopsticks.

Shinto is the old Japanese religion that taught that the emperor was a descendent of the sun-goddess. Shinto is still practiced in Japan, as well as Buddhism, and there are many Shinto shrines in the country.

Shut away from other countries for centuries, the Japanese lived in a feudal society until the middle of the nineteenth century. In a feudal society a lord owned land and let vassals use the land. In return, the vassals gave services, like military services, to the lord. A few traders and missionaries came, but made little difference to this way of life.

---

left: The Ginza section of Tokyo with its neon signs and stores always seems busy.

More than a hundred years ago, an American naval officer named Commodore Perry went to Japan and tried to get into the country. He took with him a shipload of presents for the Japanese emperor, presents such as the emperor had never seen or known before. The emperor was so pleased with the presents that he wanted to know more about the countries that could make such things. Commodore Perry suggested that the emperor start to trade with other countries. The emperor agreed, and the country was opened for trade. The eyes of the Japanese people were opened too, for until then they had had no idea of what was going on in any other country except China.

They were amazed to hear about railroad trains, the telegraph, and other marvelous machines. Then Japan sent thousands of her brightest young men to the United States and to the countries of Europe to learn about such things. When these men returned they taught their own people, who were very quick to learn. It was not long before they had copies of everything the Western world had. Japan became an up-to-date country, and in only one hundred years they jumped a thousand years ahead of the Chinese!

In return Japan gave the Western world many things to learn about and copy such as their lovely flower arrangements and gardens; origami (the art of making pictures by folding paper); block-print painting; jiu-jitsu and judo; and their love of beauty and quiet.

Many things in Japan remain as they were before the opening of the country. The landscapes, country houses, pagodas, gardens, and colored paper umbrellas are still the same.

So we can say that Commodore Perry not only opened the world to Japan but opened Japan to the world. And the world found much to admire and imitate.

One of the first things the Japanese people copied from the Western world was a baby carriage. But they designed it to carry grown-up people. In Japan they have very few horses, because horses eat too much. So an American sailor, living in Japan, made a large baby carriage for his wife that could be pulled by a man, for in Japan manpower was cheap. The Japanese called it a *jinriksha*, which means "man-pulling cart," or a pullman car. This ricksha, as it is called for short, seemed

---

opposite: Silk is washed outdoors in Japan

Pan American World Airways

such a good idea that the Japanese made thousands of them, and they are now used along with taxis or private cars, not only in Japan but in China and other countries of the East.

Baseball is a popular game in Japan. There are two leagues, the Pacific and the Central. In Tokyo, baseball is played in Korykuen Stadium. As in the United States, the Korykuen Stadium has a signboard to show a home run, but instead of lights and whistles to announce a home run, a fountain sends water into the air.

A baseball game in Japan is the same as one in the United States, with the same kind of uniforms, umpires, rules, and bat boys. There is an All-Star game each year between the two leagues, and before the game there are fireworks in bright colors. When the players march out, they are presented with a bouquet of flowers by a kimono-clad girl.

In the cities many of the people wear Western clothes, but many Japanese people, both men and women, still wear kimonos. A kimono is a loose, long gown tied around the middle with a wide sash.

There are two important holidays for Japanese boys and girls. The one for girls comes on the third day of the third month, or March 3. It is called Doll Day and the girls get out all their dolls, dress them in their finest clothes, and play with them. The one for the boys is on the fifth day of the fifth month, or May 5. It is called Flag Day or Kite Day. Big paper kites in the form of a fish called a carp are hung out on poles in front of the houses where there are boys. The carp is a fish that swims upstream against the current, which is a hard thing to do, instead of downstream, which is easy. So the carp is a model for boys—to do the hardest thing, not the easiest.

The Japanese love flowers and they have holidays when the flowers are in bloom. One holiday comes in the spring when the cherry trees, plum trees, and peach trees bloom, and another comes in the fall when the chrysanthemums bloom. Every house in Japan has a garden, no matter how small it may be—a tiny imitation of the countryside—with tiny lakes and tiny mountains, and tiny rivers with tiny bridges over them, all so perfectly made that a photograph of such a garden looks like a picture of real mountains and lakes and rivers—like a doll garden.

Japanese landscape gardening is an art often copied by other nations. This kind of gardening seems to come naturally to the

Japanese. Maybe this is because of the natural beauty of the landscape throughout their country. There are beautiful mountains, short spreading trees, arched bridges crossing ponds where children feed carp and goldfish, hidden valleys, and cherry trees with their soft blossoms.

Tea came to Japan from China in about 700 A.D. In the fourteenth century, a game called *tocha* (tea contest) also came from China. At a party, people would be given tea from different places and asked to name the place where the tea was grown. Anyone who guessed right would win a prize. As this game became more popular, tea became more popular.

This game gradually changed to a gathering of people who enjoyed the pleasure of tea and good company, and this in turn evolved into what is called the Tea Ceremony. Certain rules were set down to be followed at a tea ceremony. The basic tea drinking ceremony, called Chanoyu, was refined and finally perfected by a Zen Buddhist priest. The Japanese people appreciate true, natural beauty. The object of Chanoyu is to create a sense of peacefulness and beauty. The smallest rules of Chanoyu are intended to give this result.

above left: A tea ceremony in Japan

above: Japanese floral arrangement

Air France Photo

Chanoyu has been an important influence in Japanese life. Things to be considered in the tea ceremony are the room where the tea is served, the garden next to the room, the serving vessels, and the table setting. The development of architecture, landscape gardening, ceramics, and flower arrangement have all been greatly affected by this ceremony. Manners in a house, too, have come partly from the manners used in Chanoyu.

A typical ceremony now is in a tea house or Sukiya, which has a tea room, a waiting room, a garden, and a garden path. The main utensils are the tea bowl, tea caddy, bamboo tea whisk, and bamboo spoon. These usually are beautiful works of art. Usually soft colors are used in the clothing worn, and the guests bring a small fan and paper napkins.

The tea ceremony, which lasts about four hours, consists of four parts: a light meal, a short recess, then thick tea, and, finally, thin tea. Sometimes just the thin tea is served; this takes about one hour. The parts of the tea ceremony are accompanied by customs such as ringing a metal gong for the main ceremony, and the host or hostess follows certain procedures more complicated than just "pouring."

In many places, people are hired to entertain at parties. Their entertainment makes the party more enjoyable for the guests. In Japan, women called geisha girls entertain. Most of these girls are sold into training at an early age. These young girls receive training in singing, dancing, playing musical instruments, and, most important of all, in the art of conversation. They are trained to talk about the past and also about current things. They dress very well and are well mannered. The famous geisha girls are hired for large sums of money to entertain. When a geisha marries, she has to leave the profession. The ones who do not marry usually teach dancing or music, or train other young girls to be geisha girls.

In Japan there is a beautiful mountain with a snow-white top. It is the sacred mountain of Japan called Fujiyama, or sometimes just Fuji. Most of the land in Japan is mountainous. The mountains run down the center of the country and there are still some active volcanoes there. Mt. Fuji is a burned-out

left: One of the famous Geisha girls

opposite: Snow-covered Mt. Fuji towers above the land

Pacific Area Travel Association Photo

volcano, the top of which is covered with snow. You can see it from a very long way away, and the Japanese people love it. They put pictures of it on every conceivable thing they want to decorate—on fans, boxes, trays, umbrellas, lanterns, and screens. No movie queen or famous beauty has ever had as many pictures made of her as have been made of Mt. Fuji.

There is a huge bronze statue of Buddha in Japan, seated out of doors in a grove of trees. It is so large that half a dozen people can sit on its thumbs. The eyes are of solid gold and more than a yard long, and in its forehead is a large ball of solid silver. They call it the Diabutsu of Kamakura.

The Japanese people put up statues of Buddha to remind them that he was wise and good and that his life was an example that everyone would do well to imitate.

This Great Buddha is the most famous of all Buddhas and is a national treasure. The Buddha looks down at people who come to visit him. He was at first inside a wooden building, but typhoons and tidal waves ruined the building and left the Buddha for everyone to see.

Tokyo is the capital and largest city of Japan. In fact, it is one of the largest cities of the world. The old capital has exactly the same letters as Tokyo but arranged this way: Kyoto. If you say Tokyo twice you say Kyoto too—TO/KYOTO/KYO.

Tokyo today is a modern city with skyscrapers and wonderful modern buildings. There are restaurants, night clubs, theaters, and shops. In the shops you can buy brocaded silks, carved ivory, lacquer ware, and wood-block prints. Because Tokyo grew into a very large city in a very short time, there were great traffic problems. Before the Olympic Games were held in Tokyo in 1964, modern expressways and highways were built to help ease some of the traffic problems. The monorail helps commuters move easily around the city.

One of the principal streets of Tokyo is Ginza, where there are large stores and offices and many neon signs. Tokyo also has old sections where many of the buildings are built of bam-

opposite: The Great Buddha of Kamakura

boo. The sea serpent is still shaking himself nearly every day. When a bad earthquake comes—and slight ones come almost every day and terrific ones every once in awhile—the old bamboo buildings can be destroyed. The buildings sometimes are toppled, as if they were toy blocks; but the chief damage done by an earthquake is from the fires that start when lights and stoves are upset. In these fires, thousands of houses may be destroyed.

Most of the new buildings are built to withstand earthquakes. They are built on underground platforms of concrete instead of on the solid rock of the earth. This keeps them from being torn from their foundations when an earthquake shakes the ground; just as a big loose rock lying on the ground might be shaken but would not be broken apart. Tokyo plans to rebuild all the buildings to be safe from earthquakes.

Japanese houses made good bonfires, for they are not only made entirely of wood, but the windows are made of paper and the floors are covered with straw mats. The mats are not made to fit the floor, but the floors are made to fit the mats, which are all of the same size. The rooms are built to the size of six mats, ten mats, and so on. In order to keep the mats clean, the Japanese take off their shoes whenever they enter their houses, and walk about the house in their stocking feet.

There are no chairs in most Japanese houses, for the Japanese sit on the floor. The tables in a Japanese house have legs only a few inches high; they are really only trays. The meals are served by placing such a tray in front of each person as he squats on his heels on the floor. There are no beds either. The Japanese people sleep on the mats and cover themselves with a padded kimono for a comforter and use a hard wooden block for a pillow.

In large cities in Japan many of these customs have changed. If you visited a Tokyo apartment you might have to remove your shoes, but when you went inside you would probably sit on a chair and your hostess would have many modern conveniences.

The Japanese bathe frequently, using a tub shaped like a sawed-off barrel in which there is room to sit but not to lie down. The water is piping hot "to open the pores." After the bather has par-boiled himself, he then climbs out and scrubs himself.

The Japanese eat very little meat, because they have few animals such as cows, sheep, or pigs. Buddhists do not believe in eating meat anyway. But fish is not considered meat, and the Japanese catch and eat more fish than any other people in the world, even more than the people in Norway. Because Japan is made up of islands, no one lives far from the sea, and fresh fish may be had all the time. Peddlers carry live fish in tubs of water, on a pole which rests on their shoulders, so that fish will be absolutely fresh. Fish caught in Japan are sardines, herring, mackeral, yellowtail, bonito, pike, whale, tuna, salmon, and carp. Japan is the leading fishing nation in the world and has a very big fishing fleet. But rice is the chief food in Japan and tea is the chief drink. Rice is a cereal that is grown in much the same way as wheat, oats, or barley except that most of the land is covered with water while the rice is growing. Most of the planting and harvesting of rice in the Orient is done by hand and the fields where rice is grown are called *paddies*. Many dishes are prepared with rice.

High wooden gateways called *Torii* are everywhere in Japan, standing sometimes alone, sometimes in lines. Torii means "bird rest." They are sacred gateways under which one passes to a temple or shrine.

Large stone lanterns are often found around Japanese temples and in Japanese gardens. These lanterns give very little light, but they are much more ornamental than other lanterns, and the Japanese admire beauty. They even have a festival of lanterns.

There are three monkeys carved in wood in the greatest of all Japanese temples at Nikko. One monkey has his paws over his ears, the next over his mouth, and the third over his eyes, meaning: "Hear no evil, speak no evil, see no evil."

Can you picture two very fat men squatting on the ground and facing each other in the center of a huge building around which are sitting thousands of people watching?

The two fat men are wrestlers. Wrestling is a national sport in Japan. Sumo wrestling is done by huge men weighing several hundreds pounds, who wrestle before crowds of people like those that gather to watch baseball or football games. The wrestlers squat, facing each other like huge bullfrogs, and spend most of their time in this position, each watching for a chance to get a grip on the other. The game seems simply one of watching and waiting, for once one gets a "hold" on the other the battle is over.

Another kind of wrestling is called jiu-jitsu. It is trick wrestling, and a small person, if he knows how, can throw a much larger and stronger person by catching his arm, hand, or leg and twisting it with a quick movement into certain positions that are impossible to resist. In Japan whole schools sometimes line up two and two, practicing the various "throws" with lightning-like movements. Jiu-jitsu is really the art of self-defense and people in many countries study and learn this so they can protect themselves.

Kyoto, the old capital of Japan, has imperial palaces and ancient shrines. The Heian Shrine was built in 1895. This wooden house is like an extension of its garden. When the doors with the paper covers are open, the house and the garden blend perfectly together. Many houses in Japan are built in this way.

Many countries now have presidents rather than emperors, and Japan has a president now, too. Japan has a democratic form of government with a head called a prime minister. The emperor and his family still live in Japan and although they don't rule, they are respected and loved by the people in Japan.

The Imperial Palace in Tokyo is where the emperor lives. It is surrounded by a moat. The outside can be visited by tourists, but the inside is only open on special days. The royal family lives there and greets the visitors on these special visiting days.

Northwest Orient Airlines

opposite: Delicate Japanese architecture is seen in the Heian Shrine in the old capital, Kyoto

52

Map of Southeastern Asia

Burma, Thailand, Malaysia, Singapore, and Indonesia

Burma is a relatively new country, for Asia. The first king who ruled over the country was the great Anawrahata, in 1044 A.D. Kublai Khan invaded in 1287, and it was not until 1757 that another Burmese king ruled all Burma. The British conquered the country in 1885, to stop the Burmese attacks on British India. During World War II, Burma was held by the Japanese. Both sides bombed the cities and burned the farms, and the people suffered greatly. In 1948, the country became the Union of Burma, the third country in history to become completely free of the British Empire.

If you were going to Burma from India, you would go through a pass in the Chin Hills or the Naga Hills. These "hills" are really mountains, 6000 to 20,000 feet high. The Shan highlands in east Burma are only 3000 feet high. The hills and highlands have a temperate climate. Central and lower Burma are low and have a tropical climate—hot, with a long rainy season when the *monsoons* blow. Monsoons are strong winds that blow over the area around Burma, bringing heavy rains.

About eighty-five per cent of the Burmese are Buddhists. Buddhism recognizes all men as equal, and Burma has never had the caste system India does. The Burmese are generally small, slender people, and most still wear their native dress. Men and women both wear the *longyi*, a long wrap-around skirt of cotton, nylon, or silk. A man's *longyi* may be solid color, striped, or plaid. A woman's is more likely to be of gaily colored flower print. Women wear a short blouse, an *aingyi*, over the *longyi*. The *aingyi* is generally white and sheer. Men used to wear the same sort of blouse, but in the cities they now wear a Western type shirt and coat over the *longyi*. Women wear their hair long, often coiled on the top of the head. They often circle the coil with fresh flowers.

Because devout Buddhists wish to reach *Nirvana*, a state of perfection, they give money to the poor. If they are wealthy, they build *pagodas*. If they are not wealthy, they buy small packets of thin gold leaves that they give to the pagodas. This gold leaf is used to decorate the pagodas, and Burmese pagodas are a glorious sight.

The largest pagoda in Burma is the Shwe Dagon Pagoda in Rangoon. The original pagoda was only twenty-seven feet high. But many rulers wanted to reach Nirvana, and they enlarged it and raised it. It is now 326 feet high. It is built on a circular platform, surrounded by a low wall. The central pagoda contains eight hairs from Buddha's head, the only relics that can still be traced back to Buddha. The pagoda is completely covered with gold leaf up to its spire. On top of the spire is a solid gold flower bud, almost completely covered with jewels. At the base of the pagoda are four chapels, with large statues of Buddha. Many smaller pagodas and shrines are scattered over the platform.

Rangoon is the capital of Burma and has large governmental offices built by the British. About 800,000 of the 22,000,000 Burmese live in Rangoon. Most of the other people are farmers and live in small villages. Although Burma is the world's leading producer of teak, only about 80,000 people actually work at lumbering. Teak is a very heavy wood, and elephants are used to move the logs. The elephants work only about five hours every day. If the drivers try to make them work longer, the elephants get angry and refuse. Burmese is the language of the elephant drivers throughout Asia—even in India, Thailand, or other countries.

In the center of Burma, northeast of Rangoon, is Inle Lake. The Inthas, a primitive tribe, live around this large, shallow lake. They build houses out over the lake on stilts. The Inthas are famous as "leg-rowers." The rower stands in the stern of the teak dugout canoe. He balances on one leg, and curves the other leg around his paddle, kicking the canoe through the water very rapidly.

Mandalay is a city of about 200,000. It is a relatively new city, first built in 1856–57 by King Mindon. He made Mandalay the capital. This fulfilled a prophecy made by Buddha 2000 years earlier. The Zegyo Bazaar in Mandalay is thronged with people from all over Burma. Here are wealthy women wearing the lovely native costume, as well as men and women from the hill tribes. If you are lucky, you may see some Pagaung women, with their long necks, stretched by wearing many brass rings around them. They also wear brass rings on their lower legs. Other women walk stiffly through the bazaar, unable to bend their knees because of the lacquered cord wound tightly around their legs. Visitors to the bazaar can buy cotton or silk cloth made by the famous Burmese handweavers, as well as packets of gold leaves to apply to pagodas and "earn merit" toward Nirvana.

Burma is very important to the rest of Asia because it grows so much more rice than it needs. We have talked about parts of Asia that do not have enough food, but in Burma there is more rice than the people who live there can eat. So, of course, Burma sells the excess to other countries in Asia. Much of Burma is dense jungle because men have not needed to clear and cultivate the land.

It is not easy to come into Burma, for much of the country is surrounded by rugged mountains that are very thick with trees. Getting through these mountains is very difficult. Only people who are well equipped to do it can make the journey.

Both the land and the climate of Burma are ideal for raising rice. One stretch of land in Burma is called the "Paddy Zone," because the whole area is so good for developing rice paddies. The land in the Paddy Zone is very flat, and the area gets much heavy rain and very hot sun. The various rivers in the area deposit earth as they flow along and keep the soil very fertile. This is something like what the Nile River does in Egypt, but on a much smaller scale.

Burma is also suitable for raising what are called "dry land crops." These are food crops, but not rice. The Paddy Zone is in the coastal areas, the dry land crop zone is inland.

As you might expect when you see that Burma is on the sea, fishing is one of the resources that makes Burma important. You might also expect that all the trees on the mountains would be another source of wealth. But this is not so in Burma because the trees are located in a place that is hard to reach. You can't use trees if you can't get to them easily.

Much of Burma is as yet undeveloped. The Burmese have not had much contact with the outside world and so have done things a little differently; they have not yet become a complete part of the modern world. For awhile, Burma was under the control of the English, and they learned from them a lot about developing the land.

Southeast of Burma is Thailand, a country whose name means "Home of the Free." Thailand is, indeed, the home of the free, for it is the only southeast Asian country that was

American President Lines

never a colony of a European nation. Most Thais still wear the *pasin*, a long cloth skirt wound around the waist and held by a belt, and woven straw hats that look like lampshades. Women wear a blouse called the *sabai chiena*, which leaves one shoulder bare. Materials used are brightly colored cotton or the magnificent handwoven Thai silk. Many wealthy Thais now wear Western clothes.

Thailand is a tropical country, and about seventy per cent of the land is covered with heavy forests. The southern forests are thick jungles, with many rubber trees. Teak grows in the northern forests where elephants are used in harvesting. Teak is a valuable wood, and is used by Thai craftsmen for the handles of their beautiful bronze tablewear. Northeast Thailand is a largely unfertile plateau where little can grow, but the flat plain in central Thailand is very fertile and rice is raised there.

Thai women are small and delicate-looking. Many girls study the classical Thai dancing in Bangkok, the capital. Each gesture of a dancer's hands has a special meaning, and Thai audiences sit spellbound before dance dramas that sometimes last as long as four hours.

Kite flying is a serious sport in Thailand. Thais are as interested in kite-flying contests as other countries are in baseball, football, or soccer games. Boys watch the men fly the big kites that require four or five men to handle, and practice with their own smaller models. A team flying a star-shaped *chula* (male kite) tries to bring down the long-tailed *pakpa* (female kite).

Bangkok, the capital, is a city of over 1,000,000 people. *Krung Thep*, its Thai name, means "City of Angels," and Bangkok does seem favored by angels. It is a beautiful, happy city, where even the poor seem to have enough to eat and wear. Canals cut through Bangkok, and almost half the people live and work on houseboats, called *sampans*, sometimes never

Pan American World Airways

opposite: Siamese dance troupe performs a classical dance

above: Shopping area in Bangkok, Thailand

above: A floating market in Bangkok

above: Elephants are used for rolling teak in Bangkok

above: Valuable teak wood
comes from this tree

opposite: Wat Arun, the
Temple of the Dawn, Bangkok

going ashore. They fish or market the produce brought in by farmers. The floating markets of Bangkok provide a colorful display of coconuts, mangoes, and other tropical fruits and vegetables. Houses built on stilts line the edges of the canals. Wealthier Thais live in large Thai houses.

Up until 1939, Thailand was known as Siam. We often think of Siamese cats when we think of Siam, but there are no longer any of these blue-eyed, hoarse-voiced cats in Thailand. The Thais will tell you, with twinkling eyes, that all the cats have gone to live in England and the United States.

There may be no more cats in Thailand, but there are elephants who work in the teak forests. There are monkeys of many kinds. In the southern forests, monkeys are trained to throw coconuts down from the trees. There are other animals, too. Because most Thais are Buddhists, they do not hunt these animals, but other people organize safaris into the jungles, looking for tigers and rhinoceros.

Every Thai man spends at least three months of his life in a Buddhist monastery. No matter how poor or how wealthy his family, even if he comes from the royal family, in the monastery he wears a simple yellow robe. Every morning at dawn the monks go out with their empty begging bowls. The monks hold out their bowls silently, and the people put food in the bowl. As a person gives the food he thanks the monk, for the giver of food has "gained merit" by his charity.

Thailand is an unusual Asian country because food is plentiful. The rivers and canals teem with fish. Thailand is one of the world's leading rice exporters. Rice is grown in the central area on small farms, planted and tended with primitive farming tools. Thai food is delicious. Some of it is like Chinese food and some is like the curries of India. But all of it is very good.

There are more than 400 *wats*, or Buddhist temples, in Bangkok. The most famous wat in Thailand is the Temple of the Emerald Buddha. This temple is the royal chapel and is part of the Grand Palace in Bangkok. The Emerald Buddha itself is carved out of one piece of green jasper (not emerald), and is thirty-one inches high. Priests change the special gold and jeweled garments three times a year—at the hot, cold, and rainy seasons.

(text continued on page 81)

Makeup identifies good and evil characters in Peking Opera.
Each district in China has its own kind of opera.

The Globe and Mail, Toronto—Photo by Charles Taylor

The Globe and Mail, Toronto—Photo by Charles Taylor

Everyone enjoys parades and holidays in Peking, China.
Bright colors are used to liven the celebrations.

Many Oriental families spend much
of their lifetime on sampans which are
both homes and workshops

Bob Brunton—Hollis Associates

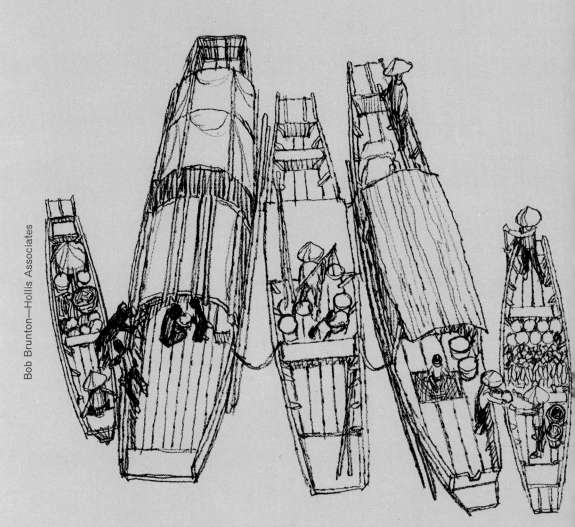

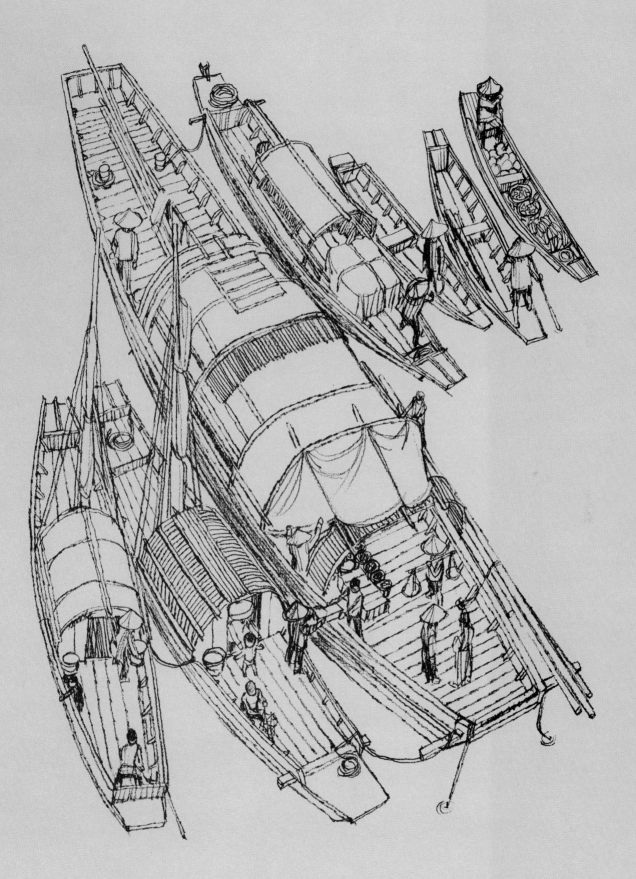

Ta Yu Ling, the
highest point
on the East-west
Cross-island
Highway, Taiwan

Pacific Area Travel Association Photo

Ifugao Rice Terraces.
Like gigantic stairways to
the sky, these marvels of
ancient engineering in the
Philippines were carved
out of the mountainsides
by Ifugao tribes
thousands of years ago
at heights of 5000 feet.

left: The natural beauty of the
Japanese countryside
near Hakone

above: Shrimp divers,
mostly young women, work along
the shore of Japan

above: A street lined with shops in the old section of Hong Kong.

right: Boats with decorated sails anchor in the harbor of Hong Kong

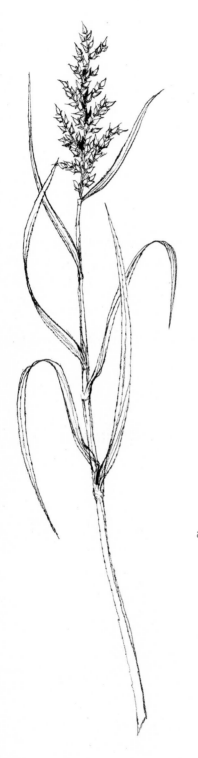

left: The rice plant,
the source of
the main food used
in the Orient

---

right: Rice sheaves
are ready for bundling
and transplanting,
Thailand

below: Commercial fishing off Kaikoura coast
on the South Island of New Zealand

right: The native policeman in Suva, Fiji,
wears a skirt called a sulu

left: Native girls from the
island of Bali, Indonesia

(text continued from page 62)

Malaysia is a country separated into two parts by about 400 miles of the South China Sea. Mainland Malaysia is on the Malay peninsula, south of Thailand, and has a coastline of over 1000 miles. A mountain range runs down the center of the peninsula, with mangrove swamps on the west coast and sandy beaches on the east. About eighty per cent of mainland Malaysia is thick jungle, and only subsistence farming is done. Subsistence farming gives just enough food to live on. Rubber trees are cultivated in plantations, and rubber is the most important export. Malaysia is also the world's largest producer of tin.

The states of Sarawak and Sabah are on the island of Borneo. The coastal plain of Sarawak is dotted with mangrove swamps and cut by rivers draining from the jungle-covered hills. Sabah has only a narrow coastal plain, rising rapidly into mountains. Mt. Kinabula (13,455 feet high), the highest point in Malaysia, is here. Both mainland Malaysia and the island states have a hot, humid, tropical climate.

The strength, and also the weakness, of Malaysia is the differences in her people. Slightly less than forty per cent are Malay. About forty-two per cent are Chinese. Indians and Pakistanis number about ten per cent. The rest are a number of different peoples.

Malay is the official language, and is spoken by all those who are Malay. These people are Moslems, and follow Islamic religious and food customs. The Chinese who live in Malaysia originally came from south China and speak many Chinese dialects, as well as Mandarin. Mandarin is the dialect that was used by the imperial Chinese court. It is the language of Chinese literature and is spoken by educated Chinese. The Chinese are Buddhist, Confucians (followers of Confucius), and Taoists (followers of Lao and Tse). They are the traders and merchants of Malaysia and live mostly in the cities. Most of the Indians are Hindus from south India who speak Tamil. All three major groups tend to keep within their own group, and there has been little intermarriage. The groups regard each other with suspicion, and this sometimes leads to government problems because of language differences. English also is used as an official language.

Food in Malaysia reflects the three main cultures. Chinese dishes and Indian curries are popular. A native Malay dish is *satay*, chunks of meat dipped into a spicy sauce and then

---

opposite: A Chinese Temple Pagoda in Penang, Malaysia

grilled over charcoal. Even the food is rarely a common bond. Chinese dishes are based largely on pork, which the Moslem Malays are forbidden to eat. Malay satays are usually beef— which the Hindus cannot eat. Fish is widely used by all three peoples, as is lamb. Orthodox Buddhists, of course, are vegetarians.

Kuala Lumpur, the capital of Malaysia, is a city of about 500,000. It is about twenty-eight miles from the west coast, at the point where the Klang and Gombark rivers meet. The name itself means "muddy mouth," referring to the rivers. The king, or *Yang di-Pertuan Agong*, and his court live at Kuala Lumpur and the Houses of Parliament are here. The National Museum has a complete Chinese house built inside, as well as displays showing a Malay royal wedding, classical dances, top-spinning, and many other things.

Traditional Malay culture is still found in the villages, particularly in the northwest, where men and women still wear the Malay sarong. In the state of Kelantan, men still have top-spinning contests, as well as kite-flying contests.

Malaysia was formed as a federation in 1963 when Malay, Singapore, Sarawak, and Sabah were united. The Federation is not recognized by either Indonesia or the Philippines, although the Philippines trade with Malaysia.

In August, 1965, the state of Singapore withdrew from the Federation and became independent. The city of Singapore is the fourth largest port in the world. It is truly a "melting pot" city, with almost every Asian nation represented in its people.

About seventy-seven per cent of the 1.8 million people in the state are Chinese. Official languages of Singapore are English, Chinese, Malay, and Tamil.

The city was founded in 1819 by Sir Stamford Raffles of the British East India Company. It is named after an earlier city, *Singapura*, the Lion City, which was destroyed by the Javanese in 1377. Singapore is the most important port in southeast Asia, and handles all the tin, rubber, and other raw materials exported from Malaysia. Although the most important activities are concerned with the exporting of raw materials or importing of finished goods, Singapore also has factories for making rubber and smelting tin. Some food is grown on the island, but most is imported.

opposite: A section of Kuala Lumpur, capital of Malaysia

British Overseas Airways Corporation

Indonesia stretches over the largest island group in the world—3000 islands scattered over 3000 miles of ocean. These islands were long known to Europeans as the Spice Islands, because most of the world's exotic spices came from the Molucca Islands. The early explorers of the Western Hemisphere—from Christopher Columbus on—were looking for an easier sailing route to the Spice Islands, not looking for North or South America.

The five largest islands are Sumatra, Java, Borneo, Sulawesi, and West Irian. On the north of Borneo, the states of Sarawak and Sabah are part of Malaysia. Indonesia feels that this part of Borneo should belong to Indonesia, although the people there prefer being part of Malaysia. The western half of the island of New Guinea, known at West Irian, is Indonesian. The eastern part belongs to Australia. Indonesia has threatened to take this eastern part by force, and Indonesian soldiers often stage quick raids over the border.

The large islands all have mountains in the center, rising from wide coastal plains. Java and Sumatra both have peaks over 12,000 feet high. Volcanoes are still active in the mountains. Indonesia has a wet, tropical climate. Although the mountain regions are more temperate, they also get more rain—up to 240 inches a year. The islands can be thought of as a link between Asia and Australia, and many of the plants and animals of both continents are found here.

Indonesia has ninety-seven million people; about two-thirds of them live on Java. Djakarta, the capital, is on Java, and has almost four million people. It is the most important commercial city in the islands, and most of the exports are shipped from here. These include rubber, oil, tin, tobacco, tea, and coffee.

Most Indonesians are of Malay stock. About ninety per cent of the people are Moslems. Only on the small island of Bali are most people Hindu. Bahasa Indonesia is the official language. It is a mixture of Malay, other Indonesian dialects, Dutch, English, and Arabic. English is the second language of the country and is a compulsory subject in all secondary (high) schools.

Many of the people living in Djakarta and other large cities now wear western clothes, rather than the more colorful native dress. But if you leave the cities and travel into the villages, you can still see Indonesian life as it was lived many years ago.

opposite: Rice terraces on the island of Bali, Indonesia

Coffee, tea, and rubber are grown mainly on large foreign-owned plantations. Tea is grown on mountain plantations, and the tea pickers still wear huge umbrella-shaped hats to protect themselves from the sun.

Jogjakarta, across the island from the capital, is the center of Indonesian arts and crafts. Here is the Leather Institute, where puppets for shadow dramas are made from animals' hides; the Bamboo and Ceramic Institutes; and the Batik Institute. Batik is an Indonesian cloth, made of cotton and treated with hot wax and then dyed. The portion covered with wax does not become colored, and elaborate designs are made by covering different portions of the cloth with wax and then dyeing them with different colors. It is a long, hard process, and each section of Indonesia has different designs.

The small island of Bali is one of the most beautiful in the world. Volcanoes in the mountains are still active, and in 1963 Gunung Agung erupted for the first time in 100 years, destroying much property and claiming many lives. The Balinese are Hindu, and are gifted artists who do carving in wood as well as work in gold and silver. Balinese dancers are world famous and each movement of hands or bodies has a meaning that is understood by their audience. Here are elaborately carved temples and brilliantly dressed women. The Balinese mark all the important events in their lives with a celebration. Wedding ceremonies and birth ceremonies are colorful. But the most elaborate are the cremation ceremonies, for the Balinese believe that burning the body after death frees the soul for a future life. Highly ornate cremation towers, eighty feet high, take months to build. The bodies are laid inside these towers, which are then carried in procession on the shoulders of many men to the place where the towers are burned, amid much rejoicing.

Sumatra is considerably larger than Bali. Its people are farmers and in each district the people dress differently and have different customs. Sumatra, too, has mountains, but also many low-lying places. Palembang is fifty miles from the sea, but still at sea level. Most of the houses are built on piles above the canals and rivers of the city. In the mountains, Lake Toba at 3250 feet is surrounded by higher mountain peaks.

---

opposite: Balinese women carrying straw baskets on their heads

Laos, Cambodia, North Viet Nam, and South Viet Nam

Laos is a rugged, mountainous country, completely landlocked. In the north, mountain peaks tower more than 8000 feet. Only three passes in the Annam Cordillera allow passage into Viet Nam. The south, near Cambodia, is somewhat lower, and is dominated by the Mekong River. This river forms the border between Thailand and Laos, and eventually flows through Cambodia into South Viet Nam.

Almost two-thirds of Laos is covered with forests, and lumbering is an important industry. Much of the northern forests are teak, and here the elephants labor to bring the logs to the sawmills. In the south, bamboo and palms are found, and oxen, as well as elephants, are used. So important are elephants to Laos that an elephant is shown on the modern flag.

The people are related to the Thai people, and the Laotian language is similar to Thai. French is used as the second official language, but English is also used as a second language.

Most of the lowland Thai people are Buddhists, and Buddhist temples are found everywhere. The mountain tribes are still animists. Animists believe that the *phi* (spirit), rule a person's life. Earth, sky, fire, water, jungle, and every animal, as well as each person, has its own special phi. The Laotians believe that there are many evil phi, who must be offered sacrifices so they will not harm anyone. Even the lowland people cling to some of these beliefs, weaving them in with Buddhism, the state religion.

Laos is a constitutional monarchy, with both a royal capital, Luang Prabang, and an administrative capital, Vientiane. The French established a protectorate over Laos in 1893 and ruled the area until the Japanese invasion in 1945. After World

left: A Balinese Temple, Indonesia

War II, there were a number of revolts against the French, and Laos became an independent country within the French Community of Nations in 1949. Communist forces from North Viet Nam, the Viet Minh, invaded Laos in 1953 and the Laotian Pathet-Lao joined them. After much fighting, an agreement was signed in Geneva in 1962, which called for all foreign troops to leave. But there has been some fighting in the area at times ever since.

Almost ninety-five per cent of Laotians are farmers, mainly doing subsistence farming. Rice is the most important crop, and fish from the Mekong and other rivers is the most important source of protein. There is some animal raising, but most people get no meat to eat.

Few Laotians go to school, and less than one-third of the people can read or write. The country still has many tropical diseases, malaria being the greatest problem, and there is a high death rate for infants and young children.

Cambodia is south of Laos, a kingdom of about 67,000 square miles stretching between Thailand and South Viet Nam. This is the remaining portion of the vast Khmer Empire, which stretched across southeast Asia 700 years ago. Mountains separate Cambodia from Thailand, but the central plain is low and fertile. Here are the *Tonle Sap* (Great Lake) and the Mekong River. During the rainy season, the Mekong overflows, and makes the Tonle Sap increase from about 100 square miles to almost 800 square miles. Most of the Cambodians live near the rivers or the Tonle Sap.

Rice is both the most important part of the Cambodian's diet and also the country's main export. Although about three-quarters of the country is covered with forests and jungles, little lumbering is done. Rubber, however, is grown and exported.

Most Cambodians are descendants of the Khmers. Buddhism is the state religion, but as in Laos the people are animists as well. Cambodian is the national language and is spoken by about five million of the over six million people. French is the second language.

The Khmer Empire has long since passed, but Angkor Wat deep in the Cambodian jungles gives an idea of the greatness of this empire. Ancient palaces and temples are all that remain of a city abandoned at the height of its power. No one has yet figured out why Angkor Wat was deserted, seemingly without reason.

Pan American World Airways

left: Idols of the lost city of Angkor, Cambodia

opposite: Part of the ruins of the Temple of Angkor, Cambodia

Bob Brunton

The French established a protectorate over Cambodia in 1863 and retained it until 1946. In 1953 Cambodia finally became independent of France, and is now an elective, constitutional monarchy. King Sihanouk, who gained independence for Cambodia, abdicated in favor of his parents in 1955. When his father died, in 1960, the former king became Chief of State. The government claims to be neutral in politics, but leans more closely to the Chinese Communists' viewpoint than to that of the West. There have been "border incidents" with both Thailand and South Viet Nam, with each side accusing the other of raiding the other's territory. Cambodia broke off diplomatic relations with Thailand in 1961 and with South Viet Nam in 1963.

North Viet Nam is separated from Laos by the Annamite Cordillera, or mountain range. The Red River Delta in the north, the most heavily populated part of North Viet Nam, is less than ten feet above sea level. Hanoi, the capital, is on the Red River, and has about 650,000 people. In all of North Viet Nam, there are about 16,000,000 people. Most of these are a mixture of Chinese and Thai, but there are also Chinese from China living there. Vietnamese is the official language. It was previously written in Chinese characters, but now is written in Roman letters. About one-third of the words are derived from Chinese. The religious practices are those of China, being a mixture of Buddhism, Taoism, and Confucianism. The mountain tribes are animistic.

The Vietnamese came originally from southern China in the fourth century, B.C. They moved southward into what is now Viet Nam, and conquered and intermarried with the Malay tribes they found there. China conquered the entire area in 111 B.C., and held it for a thousand years. The long Chinese conquest had a strong influence on the customs of the Vietnamese, who have much more in common with China than does any other country in southeastern Asia. Native rulers slowly conquered what is now South Viet Nam. But there were long periods when the country was split into two sections.

The French came into the area, beginning in 1786, and governed all of it by 1884. The Japanese occupied the area during World War II. The Viet Minh, Communist-controlled forces led by Ho Chi Minh, took over the government in 1945. When the French returned later that year, a long struggle began. It was

92

ended with the Geneva agreement of 1954, signed by France and the Viet Minh. This agreement divided Viet Nam along the 17th parallel, and provided for elections two years later to see if the country should be re-united. The South Vietnamese refused to sign the agreement because they felt that it was unfair, because the Viet Minh would have two years in which to influence people in the more populated north.

In 1960, the Communist Viet Minh began supplying aid to the Viet Cong in South Viet Nam.

South Viet Nam is dominated by the Mekong River Delta, and is one of the most fertile rice-growing areas in the world. Farther west and south, there is a high plateau, covered with tropical evergreen forests. Elephants, tigers, deer, and buffalo roam the forests. In the delta areas, there are wide grassy plains.

South Viet Nam has about fourteen million people. Saigon, the capital is on the Saigon River, and has about one and a half million people. The people and language of South Viet Nam are the same as in North Viet Nam.

The Viet Cong, South Vietnamese rebels led by Communists and aided by the North, have been fighting since the division of the land. Many leaders have been overthrown and trouble has occurred between the government and the Buddhist religious leaders. South Viet Nam, aided by the United States, continues to fight the Viet Cong.

opposite: A Viet Cong soldier

above: South Viet Nam armored patrol craft in the Mekong Delta

93

The Republic of the Philippines

You remember we said that one of the largest groups of islands, called the Philippines, once belonged to the United States. Now it is a free nation. About seven thousand islands make up the Republic of the Philippines. Many of these islands are so small they don't even have names. Most of the large islands have mountains that are volcanoes. But many of the volcanoes are not active.

Except in the mountains, the temperature in the Philippines is warm all year. In the tropical forests, vines and climbers can be found going round and round the trees.

The large island where most of the people live is called Luzon. And, although Quezon City on Luzon is the official capital, most of the government offices are found in Manila. Manila is the most important city in the Philippines. The Santo Tomas Univeristy, founded in 1611, is a very old and important university in Manila.

Most of the other old buildings were destroyed in World War II. Many battles were fought in the Philippines during World War II and one island near Luzon, Corregidor Island, has many remains of the war. Corregidor Island can be reached from Manila on a hydrofoil boat that skims over the water at very fast speeds.

The Spanish first controlled the Philippines. Knowing that both the Spanish and the people of the United States once controlled it, you can understand why two of the three languages of the Philippines are Spanish and English. The third official language is Tagalog. It is the language taught in the schools. The Spaniards not only left their language in the Philippines, they also left their religion. Most of the people in the Philippines are Roman Catholic. The Philippines is the only Roman Catholic nation in this part of the world.

The Pagsanjan River on Luzon has jungle-filled cliffs. There are many falls where the river spills down over the rocks. It is not the best river to travel on but it is very beautiful to look at. The natives and visitors who go for canoe rides on the river come to rapids many times during their trip. Rapids are places in a river where the water goes very fast. If the people are going upstream when they come to rapids, they must get out of the boat and pull it through the water. If they are going downstream, they can "shoot the rapids," which is something like riding a roller coaster and must be very exciting.

opposite: Lake Taal, near Manila on the Philippine Islands

American President Lines Photo

left: Pagsanjan River, the Philippines

above: Filipinos threshing rice

In the Philippines there are many birds and animals. There are pheasants, doves, parrots, many jungle birds, and megapodes, which are like wild turkeys. The Philippines also have wild hogs, deer, monkeys, and wild carabao, or water buffalo. Carabao sometimes are used for work, such as pulling carts and plowing.

Most of the people of the Philippines work on farms where tall palm trees give them many coconuts and another plant gives them hemp, which is used to make rope. The coconut palm has a tall trunk with all the leaves at the top, and in the center of the cluster of leaves grows a bunch of coconuts.

Rice paddy plowed
with a carabao
or water buffalo in
the Philippines

Soviet Asia and the Mongolian People's Republic

The Union of Soviet Socialist Republics (U.S.S.R.), called the Soviet Union or Russia, stretches across the top of Asia and covers about one third of the continent. It is the largest country on earth. Most of the people live in the part of the country that lies in Europe. This is where most of the large cities are found.

Fifteen republics make up the Soviet Union. The largest republic is the Russian Soviet Federated Socialist Republic. The part of this republic in Asia is called Siberia, which stretches up into the Arctic Circle. Here the winter temperatures sometimes reach 40° below zero or colder. The ground freezes in the cold weather and in some places it is frozen permanently below the surface. Because of this, in the summer, the top layers melt into swamps. Wonderful furbearing animals and deposits of rare metals are found in Siberia. The wealth of these deposits is just lately being developed and new cities are being built in these desolate areas.

The chief port, Vladivostok, is on the Sea of Japan. The Trans-Siberian Railroad travels from here over 4000 miles into European Russia.

The area that does not stretch into the Arctic Circle is covered with evergreen forests. Lake Baikal, the deepest fresh-water lake in the world, is in the mountains of Siberia.

Below Siberia and northwest of China, are some other Soviet Republics. These are Kazakh S.S.R., Turkmen S.S.R., Uzbek S.S.R., Tadzhik S.S.R., and Kirghiz S.S.R. The S.S.R. after each is part of the complete name. It means Soviet Socialist Republic.

These republics are the original home of the people we call Turks. These nomad tribesmen moved from this area to Iran, Afghanistan, and Turkey. Millions of Turks are still to be found here, and the area is sometimes called Turkestan.

Much of the land is desert, but there is a semiarid part where the summers are short and hot and the winters are long and

right: Map of Soviet or Northern Asia

John Hollis—Hollis Associates

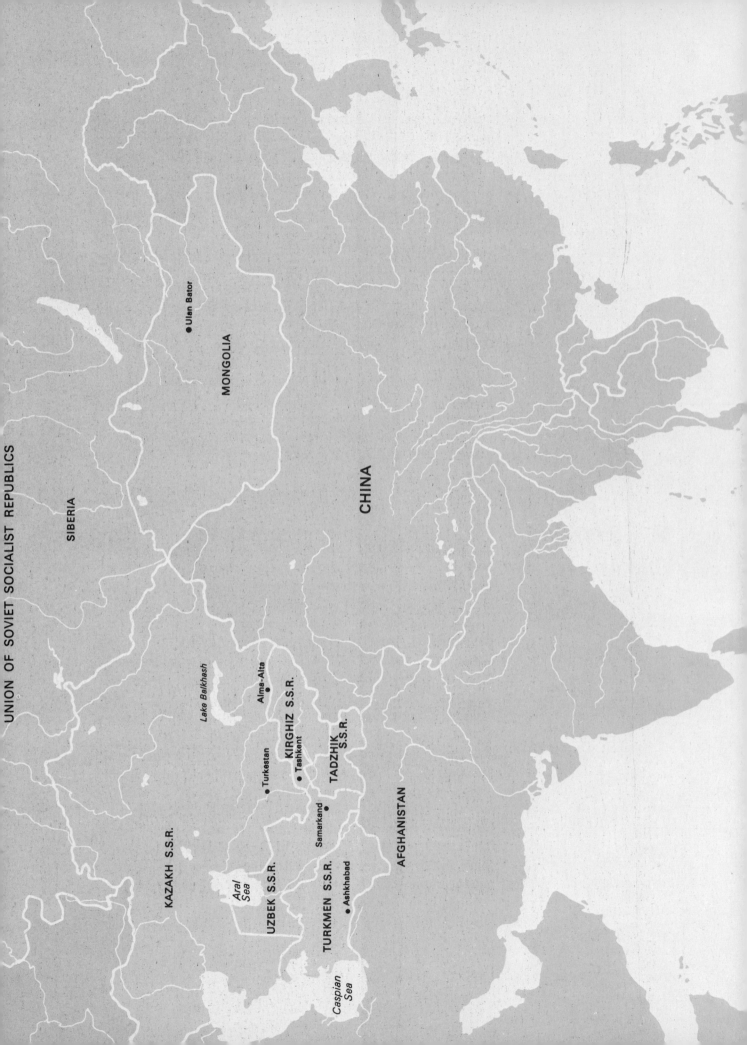

UNION OF SOVIET SOCIALIST REPUBLICS

SIBERIA

MONGOLIA

● Ulan Bator

CHINA

Lake Balkhash

KAZAKH S.S.R.

Aral Sea

Alma-Ata

KIRGHIZ S.S.R.

● Turkestan

● Tashkent

UZBEK S.S.R.

Samarkand ●

TADZHIK S.S.R.

TURKMEN S.S.R.

● Ashkhabad

AFGHANISTAN

Caspian Sea

cold with some rain or snow. Farming is done in this area and some of the finest cotton lands in the Soviet Union are here. The highest peak, Stalin Peak, 24,590 feet, is here.

The largest republic is Kazakh, where large mineral deposits are mined. Lake Balkhash, the Caspian Sea, and the Aral Sea provide fish for the canning industry. The capital is Alma-Ata.

The small republics of Kirghiz and Tadzhik are mainly rural areas where farming and cattle breeding is done.

Every year, the nomads from Afghanistan still drive their flocks into Turkmen and Uzbek and their rights are protected by treaty. Ashkhabad is the capital of Turkmen.

Most of the people in Uzbek are Moslems. Tashkent is the capital, and on Friday, you can watch the men gather here for services in the mosques. They are short, stocky people, more like the Chinese than the Arabs, with golden skin and round faces. The embroidered skullcaps of the men identify the province they come from. Men living in Tashkent, for example, decorate their caps with a row of little white cotton balls.

Tashkent has over one million people. One of the five largest textile mills in the Soviet Union is here. The Soviet government has been trying to modernize the city and make it more like European Russia. Now there are new streets and a large hotel, but the city still is more Asiatic than European. It is usually difficult for foreigners to get permission to visit Tashkent or any of the other Asiatic cities.

Samarkand has been one of the great cities of the world for thousands of years. It was an old city when Alexander the Great conquered it in 329 B.C. It was rebuilt and flourished for a long time, because it was on the old Silk Road—the overland route linking China and Europe. Genghis Khan and his Mongols swept out of Mongolia and destroyed Samarkand in 1220 A.D. Again the city was rebuilt, and in the fourteenth century Tamerlane became ruler here. Tamerlane conquered much of central Asia and gained great wealth. He used much of this wealth in rebuilding Samarkand, and it is Tamerlane's city we think of when we say "fabled Samarkand." Fifteen years before he died, Tamerlane had a magnificent tomb built for himself. Asiatic in style, its blue dome still shines in the warm sun. Soviet artists have restored the dome, but the mosaics on the pale walls have not yet been restored.

In southern Siberia, near Lake Baikel, is a section called Buryat. Most of the people who live in this part of Russia are Buddhists. These people are Mongols, descendents of the Tartars who followed Genghis Khan out of Mongolia and conquered China, most of Russia, and much of Asia. They speak Buryat—a Mongol language. The Mongols even today are nomads, following their herds of horses and sheep. They live in circular tents called *yurts*, made of felt stretched over a lattice framework. The food they eat is usually lamb, supplemented by mare's milk. The men drink *kumiss*, a liquor made from fermented mare's milk.

The Mongolian People's Republic, also known as Outer Mongolia, is about 591,000 square miles in area. It is a high plateau, generally arid. The Gobi Desert in the south extends into Inner Mongolia (China). It was in the Gobi Desert that American archaeologists found dinosaur eggs, preserved millions of years by the desert sands. Although much of Mongolia is arid, there is a deep lake here.

In all this vast area, fewer than one million people live. Ulan Bator, the capital, has about 164,000. During the summer, the towns have fewer people than in the winter, for many move their yurts onto the steppes—the high grassy plains of central Asia. The official language is Khalkha Mongolian, which is much like the language spoken in Buryat and in Inner Mongolia.

In Mongolia, most of the people are nomads. Almost all livestock belongs to cooperatives rather than to private owners. Small factories in Ulan Bator supply most of the goods needed by the nomads, particularly leather goods, shoes, boots, and felt boots. Although most of the people, even in the cities, live in yurts, apartment buildings are going up in Ulan Bator. Very few apartments are being built elsewhere.

Although the Mongolian People's Republic is an independent country, it is closely tied to the Soviet Union with trade and military aid. Communist China also trades with Mongolia, and has been trying to become more important in the government. China has always regarded Mongolia as a barrier to the expansion of the Russians into China.

Most of the people who follow any religion at all are Buddhist. Before 1930, Buddhism was very important, and there were nearly 100,000 lamas (Buddhist monks). During the 1930's, however, the government closed all the monasteries. Freedom of religion has again been guaranteed, and a few of the monasteries and temples have re-opened. But Buddhist lamas no longer participate in the government and rule the country as they did for thousands of years.

Mongolian herdsman

Australia, New Zealand, and the Pacific Islands

Australia, you remember, is a continent. What do you suppose, then, that it could have in common with New Zealand and the many very small islands in the Pacific?

All of these places have two things in common. They are all insular—even Australia may be thought of as a large island. And all of them are isolated, or far removed from other places in the world. Indonesia is insular but these islands are not isolated. They are close to Asia and are very much a part of the Orient because of their position.

The lands of Australia, New Zealand, and the Pacific Islands, however, are by themselves and are not influenced by lands close to them. They have been influenced by other places in the world, of course, because most of them were settled or taken over by people from countries of Europe or the New World.

Australia and New Zealand were settled by the British, and so they are British by tradition. Other islands in the South Pacific area have other traditions and ways of life. Also among these islands is part of the United States—Hawaii. When geographers talk about Hawaii, they usually mention it primarily as one of the United States, but it is located in the Pacific Islands.

It is difficult to divide these islands into groups. Some of them have highlands with volcanoes and hills and mountains. Some have mostly low land. Some are big and some are small. Usually, geographers talk about the high islands and the low islands, meaning those that have mountains and those that do not.

Whether an island is high or low is very important, because this determines the climate. The mountainous islands receive enough moisture for growing things, but some of the low islands do not. It is usually easier to live on the high islands than it is to live on the low islands.

Australia suffers from lack of rain. In fact, most of the land is very dry, and farmers who want to raise crops have to settle in one part of Australia. People who raise livestock settle in another place, where there is less rain. Grazing land for livestock needs less rain than farmland needs. But there are large areas in Australia that are too hot and too dry for any European to live on. These areas are wastelands where very little grows.

New Zealand is much like Australia in tradition and history but not in land. New Zealand gets a lot of rain, and agriculture

right: Map of the South Pacific

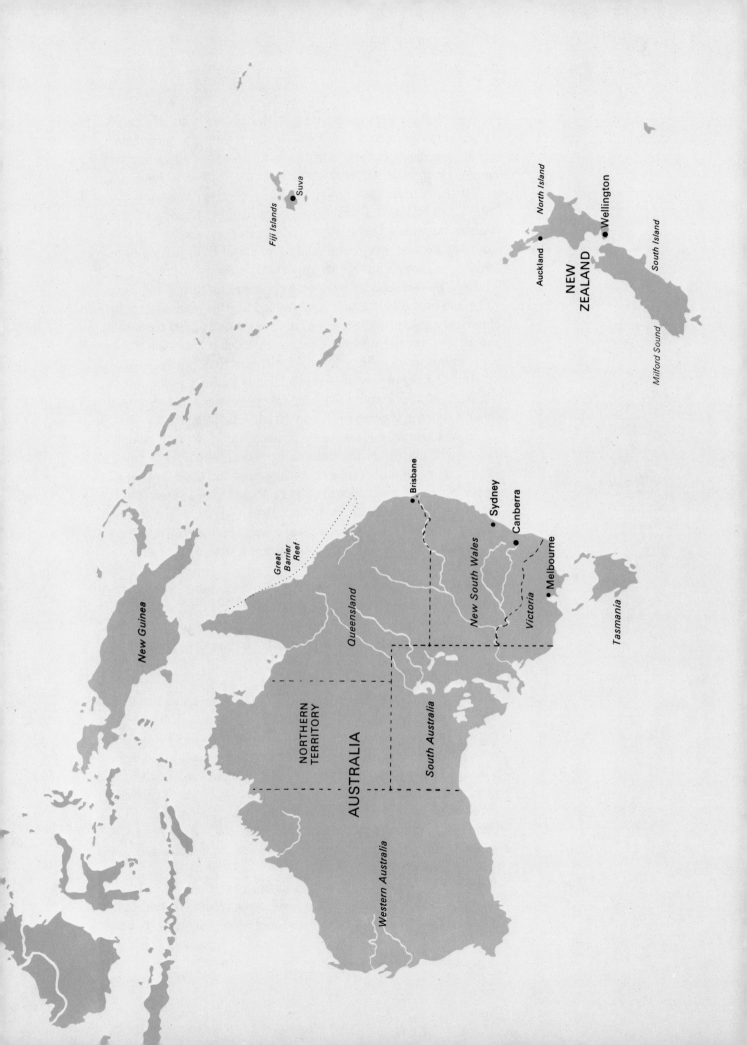

Fiji Islands

Suva

North Island

Auckland

Wellington

NEW
ZEALAND

South Island

Milford Sound

New Guinea

Great
Barrier
Reef

Brisbane

Sydney

Canberra

Melbourne

Queensland

New South Wales

Victoria

Tasmania

NORTHERN
TERRITORY

AUSTRALIA

South Australia

Western Australia

is one of the chief occupations of the people who live there. There are wastelands in New Zealand, but not dry lands. They are places where it is too cold or where there are too many swamps or where the terrain is too rugged to be useful.

Australia and New Zealand offer more than only opportunities for raising crops or livestock. Mining is important in Australia, where there is gold, silver, copper, lead, and zinc. In New Zealand are found gold, silver, and coal, among other minerals. Lumbering is also important in New Zealand.

New Zealand also has a growing manufacturing industry. The coal mined here is no longer needed for this kind of activity, for New Zealand has so much rain and such rugged mountain areas that the people can produce electricity from the power of running water. They can use hydroelectrical power.

How the people in the Pacific Islands make a living varies on each of the islands. Some of the people can make only a poor living for themselves by subsistence farming.

Subsistence farmers usually live on *atolls*, or low islands. Those who live on the high islands have better land for farming. They can raise more crops than they need for their own existence. Some of the things they raise are rice, yams, sweet potatoes, corn, bananas, breadfruit, and vegetables. In certain places they can raise tobacco also. Where there are forest areas, they can raise livestock, such as chickens, pigs, and even some kinds of cattle.

Some islands have important minerals or other natural resources that are needed in the modern world. Phosphates and guano, both used in fertilizer, are among some of the things these islands produce. Others are gold, bauxite, chromium, and nickel.

Some of the islands are important to other countries in the world for quite another reason—one that has nothing at all to do with the food or minerals that can be produced. They are important only because of where they are located. Modern transportation has made the world of today a small place. Any island that lies along a shipping route becomes important as a place where food can be stored, where fresh water can be found, or where defense weapons can be installed. Those islands that lie beneath airplane routes are important, too. Here runways can be built for landing and stations can be maintained for refueling the aircraft.

Such islands as Tutuila, which has the excellent Pago Pago Harbor, make good places for naval bases. Wake, Guam, and Midway Islands are all stepping-stones along airplane routes.

Melbourne,
the former capital city
of Australia

Kimberley region
in Western Australia

Blue Mountains,
New South Wales,
Australia

Australia, the Island Continent

As we have said, Australia is such a large island that it is called a continent. It is so far from England that it used to take five or six months to make the trip from one place to the other. Even now it takes a long time by ship. Only nomadic tribes used to live in Australia. Yet the English people went there and built great cities. Now their descendants rule over the island. They call the island–continent Australia, which means "South Land," for it is far, far south. It is south of the equator, and there it is summer when in the north it is winter, and night when in the north it is day. Many people call Australia "Down Under," because it is south of the equator. The island was so far away from England that the English thought it would be a good place to send prisoners.

It was not very long, however, before the English found that Australia was very valuable and would make a good place to live, so free settlers came from England. Australia is now a member of the British Commonwealth. It is governed by a prime minister elected by the people.

In the southeastern part of Australia the new settlers found grassland, which was good for raising sheep and cattle. But there were no sheep and no cattle. So the Englishmen sent to England for sheep and cattle. But when they arrived, the animals would not eat the grass—it was not the right kind! The Englishmen still were not discouraged and sent to England for English grass seed. At last they succeeded, for when the grass was planted it grew very well, and before long the sheep and cattle became very important to the economy of Australia. From the sheep they raised, the people got the finest wool in the world, very long and silky. It was shipped to England and other places to make woolen clothing, and Australia is now the greatest wool-raising country in the world.

Scattered throughout the country are great stock stations where millions of sheep are raised. Most of the sheep are raised in the east and southeast, away from the coast. These stations are so far apart that the children can't reach a school, so many of them listen to the radio for their school instruction. Every morning, instead of getting dressed and leaving the house for school, these children get dressed and turn on the radio, which they call the wireless, for their lessons. The teacher talks to them and they talk back. There is a microphone connected to the radio and the teacher expects to hear from the children. So even though they learn by listening to the radio, they must be on time, they must have their lessons prepared, and they must listen carefully in case the teacher asks a question.

Sheep-shearing time is a happy occasion. First there is hard work, for the sheep must be collected and taken into the barn and clipped of the wool that has grown so long and thick it makes them look fat. Then when all the work is done, the barn is cleared and friends and neighbors come for a party in the barn.

The cattle industry has grown to be a very big business, too, and now frozen beef and mutton are sent back to England, which hasn't nearly enough beef of its own.

The native animals of Australia are very peculiar. One curious animal is the kangaroo, an animal as big as a man. He stands on his two hind legs like a dog begging for food and uses his tail for support. His two front legs are very small and almost useless. The kangaroo doesn't run along on all fours; he jumps over the ground on his hind legs, making long hops. A baby kangaroo is called a *joey* and the mother carries him in a pocket in the skin of her stomach. This pocket is called a pouch.

The koala bear also lives in Australia. This is like a child's Teddy bear. It grows to be about two feet tall and has gray fur. When a koala bear is unhappy, it cries. These bears live in eucalyptus trees and eat the leaves. They do not drink water, because there is enough water in the leaves. Koala bears are nocturnal, which means they sleep during the day and are awake at night. When they sleep they sit huddled in branches of the eucalyptus trees. If someone tries to catch their attention and they wake, they look at the visitor and rub their eyes with their little paws and go back to sleep. Many stuffed toys are made that look like koala bears.

The platypus, one of the strangest animals in the world, lives in Australia. It is considered to be a primitive animal and has things in common with mammals, birds, fish, and reptiles. The platypus has thick fur like a mammal, and a bill and webbed feet like a duck. The male has a poison gland in a claw on one of his hind legs like some reptiles have. The female lays eggs and hatches them like a bird, and then nurses the babies like a mammal. The platypus is nocturnal, and is a very shy animal who doesn't bother anyone. The government is preserving and protecting this unusual animal.

The eucalyptus trees in Australia are also unusual, but they grow in other places, too. These trees can be used to dry up swamps. The roots absorb water like a blotter. The water is passed up to the leaves and finally released into the air. The leaves can hold a lot of water, which is why the koala bear doesn't need to drink any water. These eucalyptus trees, sometimes called gum trees, shed their bark instead of shedding their leaves.

Another tree that holds water is the "bottle tree" or *baobab*, which grows in northern Australia. The wood of these trees is soft and damp and there are hollow places at the base of the branches where water is stored during the summer. In the summer it rains in the northern part of Australia. Some trees may have eighty gallons of water stored inside to keep them alive during the winter. People or birds or animals, sometimes cut the trees open to take some of the water if they need it. The water is sweet and safe to drink.

An Australian bird called a kookaburra never sings—it laughs! The Australians call this bird with the loud laugh the laughing jackass. Maybe you have heard the song about the kookaburra in the old gum tree.

Descendents of the original tribes of Australia make up a very small part of the population. The earliest known people of a country are called *aborigines*. Some of the Australian aborigines can't even count up to ten or write their names or read a single word. They wear very little clothing. Instead of wearing clothes they paint their bodies; they also raise bumps on their skin by scratching it with the edge of a shell and rubbing clay into the scratches. These marks are like tattoos. The more bumps they have on their bodies, the more beautiful they think they are.

opposite top: A kangaroo holds her joey in her pouch

opposite bottom: Baobab tree found in northern Australia

The aborigines use a peculiar thing called a boomerang. It is made of a piece of wood shaped like a new moon. They throw the boomerang into the air away from themselves, and it turns round and round like a wheel and then comes back to the thrower. This is used for hunting. If the boomerang is aimed correctly, it will hit and stun an animal. If it doesn't hit the animal, it comes back and can be tossed again.

Most of the Australian aborigines live in the North and move around like a nomadic race. They know the territory very well and are able to find people who have become lost. Some of the aborigines are now employed to take care of sheep or cow herds. They are gradually becoming more a part of the rest of Australian society. This is done mainly through education.

Many of the aborigines still live in tribes, which have the same kinds of laws and rules that other societies have. In some tribes, the mother is punished whenever her child does something naughty. This makes the mother very careful to raise her children properly.

Spears, boomerangs, and bark carvings made by the aborigines can be seen in museums in Australia or bought as souvenirs.

There are six states in Australia. They are Queensland, New South Wales, Victoria, South Australia, Western Australia, and Tasmania, which is an island. Two territories on the continent are the Northwest Territory and the Capital Territory. The northwestern part of Australia looks toward Asia, but the rest of the country is surrounded by ocean. Even though it is new and so far away from everything, Australia is a very advanced nation.

The capital of Australia used to be a city called Melbourne. Melbourne has many lovely parks and gardens. It now is the capital of Victoria. In the Fitzroy Gardens in Melbourne stands a little cottage. This cottage was shipped piece by piece from England and was rebuilt in Melbourne. In this little cottage, Captain James Cook was born. Captain Cook was the first man to make a map of the east coast of Australia and to claim the island–continent for Britain. Other men from other countries had known Australia was there but had made no attempt to claim it for their country.

A new city, Canberra, has been built as the Capital Territory of Australia. Early in the twentieth century a world-wide competition was held for a plan for the National Capital. Many city planners and architects entered their ideas and a man from Chicago, Illinois, won. Walter Burley Griffin designed a beautiful and useful city with a series of lakes in the center. This city has tree-lined streets and many parks and beaches. Because it is so new, Canberra contains some of the best features of other cities in the world. It is a beautiful city, for in the background are the Australian Alps, and in the spring, the trees lining the streets blossom brilliantly.

The chief city in Australia is Sydney. It is the capital of New South Wales and is where most of the people live. Sydney Harbor is spanned by the beautiful Sydney Harbor Bridge. The harbor has deep water so any ship may enter and dock. Along the coast there are many surfing beaches famous for their highly trained and skilled lifeguards. These guards are trained not only in saving a person who is having trouble keeping afloat, but in watching for sharks, warning the bathers if sharks are near, and driving out any sharks that do come near the beaches.

Modern apartment buildings overlook the harbor and the beaches along the coast. From these apartments there is a beautiful view of the blue ocean and sky during the day and the lights of the city at night.

In Sydney you can see musical comedy, drama, ballet, opera, and concerts given by the Sydney Symphony Orchestra and visiting musicians.

In King's Cross there are coffee bars, pleasant little shops, continental restaurants, and a fountain that looks like a giant sparkler.

Hyde Park has formal avenues, fountains, flower gardens, and little tables where afternoon tea is served. In the Domain, another park, soap-box orators speak under the giant fig trees.

Near the law courts during the week lawyers in wigs and gowns can be seen talking or hurrying to court.

The place for skiing is Cooma in New South Wales. From June to September the Australian Alps are covered with snow,

top: Captain Cook's Cottage, Melbourne, Australia

bottom: Sydney Harbor Bridge, Australia

opposite: The natives or aborigines of Australia

Beach on the Great Barrier Reef, Queensland

and thousands of people come for skiing, hiking, and tobogganing.

The seasons in the northern hemisphere are just the opposite from the seasons in the southern hemisphere. When it is warm in the northern hemisphere, the countries in the southern hemisphere—at least the ones that have seasonal changes—are having winter. This is what happens in parts of Australia, but there are some parts of the country that have very little change in season. They are the tropics in the state of Queensland. In the northern hemisphere the warm places are in the *south* near the equator. In Australia it is the opposite and the warm places are in the *north* close to the equator.

Queensland is called the Sunshine State and has miles and miles of golden beaches. The capital and chief port is Brisbane. There are tropical islands off Queensland with beautiful orchids, birds with bright feathers, sugar cane farms, and crocodiles. Some of these are coral islands. These coral islands are part of the Great Barrier Reef—the longest and most breathtaking coral reef in the world. This reef is made of brightly colored skeletons of sea animals that have piled up through the years.

Australians are very much interested in sports. People go to see football games, tennis matches, cricket games, and horse racing. Australia has had many world champions in recent years in tennis, long-distance running, and swimming. Most of the players are amateurs who do not make a living by playing a particular sport.

One of the biggest problems faced by Australia is lack of water. Much of the land is not used because there is no water for irrigation. Of all the continents, Australia is the driest and there are very few rivers. During the dry weather some lakes and rivers disappear entirely. Near Canberra is Lake George, which is sometimes filled with enough water for boat races to be held on it, and sometimes so dry the cattle graze on its bottom! The rivers that supply water are in the southeastern part of the country, where most of the people live. Here many dams have been constructed to regulate the flow of water and irrigate many acres of land.

Although Australia is very large, it has only as many people as Peru, in South America. Much land is available, but without water the land is useless. When we learn how to change sea water into fresh water, Australia will have much useful land and will grow very rapidly.

115

New Zealand

New Zealand is southeast of Australia. It is really two big islands that look something like Italy, or a boot turned upside down. On the map they do not appear to be far away from Australia, but it takes a few days to get to them by ship from Australia. In the northern part of New Zealand live people called Maoris. The Maoris are quite different from the aborigines in Australia. The Maoris had a well-ordered society when the first settlers came to New Zealand. They resisted the settlements being made and have probably fared better than any other native tribe against settlers. There was a war between the Maoris and the settlers about twenty years after the first attempt at colonization. Because the Maoris fought for their rights, many of them now live side by side with the settlers and their descendants.

Both islands have mountains. On the North Island the mountains are not very high, but there are three active volcanoes. There are hot springs and geysers there too. The South Island has higher mountains called the Southern Alps.

New Zealand is popular for fishing. Almost every lake, river, and stream has fish to be caught. You can even take a boat out for big game fishing off the coast of the North Island.

In the South Island there is an area of thick forests, snow-covered mountains, swift rivers, waterfalls, and fiords. A fiord is an inlet of the sea protected by high cliffs. Because this area is much like the Norwegian fiords, it is called Fiordland National Park. The most spectacular fiord is Milford Sound. The water is so deep here that an ocean liner cannot anchor!

Many tourists visit New Zealand every year, not only to see the beautiful fiords, mountains, lakes, and rivers, but because they want to fish, ski, hunt, hike, golf, and go surfing. New Zealand, because of its warm temperatures and good rainfall, has good farming and grazing land. Here, as in Australia, many sheep graze on the land and wool is sent from New Zealand to many other countries.

The largest planted forest in the world is in New Zealand. A planted forest is man made. The New Zealand Forest Service controls most of the forest. When settlers first came to New Zealand there were many forests but now, because of cutting and clearing, many of the forests have disappeared. Just as animals must be protected when too many people capture and kill them, forest land must also be protected. The forest service says that a certain number of trees must be planted as other

opposite: The deep waters of Milford Sound, South Island

Pan American World Airways

above: Skiing near Mt. Cook, New Zealand

full-grown trees are chopped down. Even privately owned forests have certain rules that must be followed so that all the trees are not cut down.

Some interesting people were born in New Zealand. One is Sir Edmund Hillary who is famous because he is the man who climbed Mount Everest, the highest mountain in the world. For years mountain climbers dreamed of reaching the top of this mountain. Mountain climbing is a very hard sport and the people who practice it are very serious about it. They don't go climbing up mountains unless they study the climb and have the necessary equipment. A party of climbers went up the mountain in 1953 and Sir Edmund Hillary and his guide were the first ones to reach the top. Since then, he has tried to answer some important questions about how man lives in a high altitude.

The largest city in New Zealand is Auckland, on the North Island. Many extinct volcanoes form the foundation for this city which has two harbors and miles of parks.

Wellington, the capital, has steep hills and a good bay. You can take a cable car from the center of town to a hilltop and look down on the city and the water from Mount Victoria.

Some South Sea Islands

The Pacific Ocean is the biggest, deepest ocean of all. The Atlantic Ocean has very few islands in it—you could cross the Atlantic without seeing a single island, but in the Southern Pacific Ocean there are thousands of islands, and if you were shipwrecked there you would probably be in sight of one. Many of these islands are so tiny that they are only specks on the map, and some of them are not on the map at all.

If you could drain all the water out of the Pacific Ocean, as you drain water out of a bathtub, you would not see a level bottom—you would see thousands of mountains. These mountains were once volcanoes, but they have been drowned by the ocean. Where their tops are high enough to reach above the water you see islands. In the warm water around these islands live little sea animals called *polyps*. Their tiny little bones pile up until they reach the top of the water and form rings round these mountain tops. These we call coral islands.

People live on some of these coral islands but on others no one lives. On most of the islands a tree grows from which the native gets his food, drink, clothing, house, and furniture. This tree is the coconut palm.

Coconuts are about the size of a baby's head. There is a *shuck,* or hard shell, around the outside, and when this is taken off, the nut is inside. Strange to say, the coconut has what looks like two eyes, a mouth, and a sort of coarse brown hair. Just inside the shell of the coconut there is white coconut meat, and inside that there is a hollow center with coconut milk. The natives eat the meat of the nut as most of us would eat bread, and they drink the milk. So the coconut is like bread and milk. From the hair on the nut they make rope, string, cloth, and everything that others might make with cotton or silk or wool. From the coconut shells they make the cups, saucers, and all the other dishes they use. From the leaves of the tree they make short skirts, and the roofs of their houses. Their houses often have no sides—they have roofs of leaves held up by poles made from the coconut tree, and a floor that is raised a few feet from the ground.

When the settlers went to these islands they took diseases with them. The natives, who had never had such diseases before, caught them and many died. They did not seem able to get well even from measles.

Quantas Empire Airways Limited

above: Skillful Tahitian fishermen

Some natives live an easy life. They have no money, but they don't need any, for there is nothing to buy. They do no work, and if they want anything to eat, all they have to do is to climb a tree and get a coconut. This is easy, for the trees usually slant, and boys start at the ground and run up a tree as you might run up a slide. Most of the important islands now have some industry, even if it is only tourism.

An Englishman named Captain Cook—the same one who went to Australia—was the first person to explore these islands and write about them, so one group of islands is named after him.

Other men became interested in these islands because they found that the coconut meat could be sold in their countries for good prices, so they put the natives to work gathering coconuts. It was not necessary to pay them with money, because money meant nothing to them. They wouldn't work for a thousand dollars a day, but they would work for an inexpensive string of beads. They were very fond of jewelry, so the men paid them with glass beads or with phonographs and records to amuse them. Shredded coconut is called *copra* and is used in various ways. The coconut oil is used for making soap and a sort of butter.

Ships and steamers seldom pass many of these islands, and only at a few of the largest do they stop. Many stories have been told of men who were shipwrecked on coral reefs where no one lived, and where they lived alone and waited for years before they saw a ship and were picked up.

Many of these islands are so small that they have no names. Some of those with names that we will visit are the Fiji Islands, French Polynesia, and the American Samoan Islands.

An Englishman discovered Tahiti in 1767. A Frenchman also landed there a short time later. Cook discovered and explored some of the islands in French Polynesia and an American discovered some. Soon after that missionaries came to Polynesia and converted many natives to the Christian religion. Finally all the islands came under French control and all the natives were given French citizenship.

A volcanic island making up part of French Polynesia is Tahiti. This is the place that many people dream of going to visit. In fact, many actually do visit this island where the temperature is always warm and the beaches are beautiful. Tahiti is completely covered with green forests and flowers.

Some large passenger ships stop at the port of Papeete on trips around the Pacific or around the world. When they stop, the people give a warm welcome to the visitors. They meet the ship with flowers for the passengers, and of course have things to sell.

Polynesian women, who are thought to be very lovely, wear sarong-type dresses in bright-colored material with designs that look like the bright flowers that grow on the island. Many women tourists cannot resist the temptation to buy one of these garments and bring it home as a souvenir.

You can relax in Tahiti and enjoy the scenery and the wonderful, usually different, food. You can watch your dinner being cooked, for it is cooked outside in a hole filled with hot stones and covered with earth. It cooks very slowly, but you cannot see what it is because it is all wrapped in banana leaves. When it is brought to your table, you will taste a delicious meal of meat, vegetables, and fruit. You eat this with your fingers as the natives do.

In a ride around the island you can see black sand beaches, shiny white beaches, cliffs that drop down to the sea, waterfalls, clear blue lagoons, and fishing villages. In these villages, almost every Tahitian can use a net, a spear, or a rod to catch a fish.

Seven islands make up American Samoa. These islands are under the control of the United States, which means that the governor—who runs the islands—is appointed by the United States.

The people have been encouraged to keep their old customs, so a visitor can see tribal dances and other customs performed around the open, thatched-roof huts in the villages. There is a sword dance which is very exciting to see.

Small plantations where bananas, breadfruit, taro, papayas, pineapples, sweet potatoes, coffee, cocoa, and yams are culti-

Pacific Area Travel Association Photo

A Samoan making kava

Matson Lines

Pacific Area Travel Association Photo

above right: Samoans carry a freshly roasted pig

above: A Fiji warrior with whale's teeth for a necklace

vated provide work for many of the people. Some of the others are employed in an American-owned cannery for tuna fish, which is supplied by the Japanese fishing fleet.

If you come to American Samoa on a passenger ship, you would dock in the famous harbor of Pago Pago, which is also the capital.

The men wear a strange but comfortable-looking outfit called a *lava-lava*, which wraps around like a towel from the waist down. A cloth is usually wrapped around the waist like a belt. Because so many of these islands are very warm, this type of clothing is very sensible. Just as the people in the cold climates wear things to protect themselves from the cold, the people in the warmer climates must wear clothes to protect themselves from the heat.

More than three hundred islands make up the Fiji Islands and on more than half of them no people live. The people who do live on the Fiji Islands come from many different parts of the world. There are Indians, Europeans, Chinese, and Fijians.

The Fiji Islands are controlled by the British, as American Samoa is controlled by the United States and French Polynesia by the French. Fiji is the most important British colony in the Pacific Ocean.

Most of the people live on the large island of Viti Levu where Suva—the capital, harbor, and largest city—is located. In the market in Suva you hear many languages being spoken while you look at baskets, jewelry, mats, coconuts, rare sea shells, and the beautiful material used to make saris in India. A sari is a dress made from lovely silk that Indian women wear.

You can take a trip in a glass-bottomed boat in the harbor to see all the beautiful coral gardens under the water.

The Fijians perform a native war dance that their ancestors performed. They also have other ancient rituals. There is a ceremony in which you drink something called kava, which is made from roots. The people chant and clap their hands while the kava is being drunk.

With all these native customs it seems strange to see the island people playing sports brought by the English such as rugby, soccer, cricket, and hockey.

You can walk down little winding streets and look into the shops where you might see an Indian sitting on the floor making a pair of shoes and a little tailor shop where beautiful clothes are being made.

The policemen are a wonderful sight to see. They are usually tall with bushy hair and wear a wrap-around skirt with a scalloped hem called a *sulu*.

There are jungles in the center of the island where it rains very often. Thatched huts are built in cleared areas—the same kind of huts that have been built for hundreds of years.

Some of the kinds of food you might eat in the Fiji Islands are breadfruit, baked yams, fresh and salt water shrimp, oysters, crab, chicken, and raw fish marinated in lime juice.

On another island, you can see a firewalking ceremony. In this ceremony people walk on hot stones. A large pit is filled with stones, logs are placed over them, and a big fire is started. This fire burns for about eight hours and then the stones are raked to get a smooth surface. Then, immediately, the fire-walkers come out and walk around on these hot stones. It doesn't seem to bother them at all!

These are only a few of the islands in the Pacific Ocean, which number in the tens of thousands. The islands are often called Oceania. There are two kinds of islands, the volcanic and the coral. People have visited the islands in Oceania ever since Magellan discovered the Marianas in 1521. Many just come for a visit but some come to live.

Quantas Empire Airways Limited

A Fiji policeman

123

INDEX: *Young People's Story of the Orient, Australia, and the South Sea Islands*

Type   Century Expanded
Typesetter   American Typesetting Corporation
Printer   The Regensteiner Corporation